KU-356-379

PHOTO:- JUDGES LTD.

CLEOPATRA'S NEEDLE. SEE PAGE 158.

THE TRAVELLER'S GUIDE

from DEATH to LIFE

Compiled by

MRS. STEPHEN MENZIES

BRITISH GOSPEL BOOK ASSOCIATION,
5, Hope Way, Liverpool, 8, Eng.

City Agents : PICKERING & INGLIS :
14, Paternoster Row, London ;

229, Bothwell Street, Glasgow ;
29, George IV Bridge, Edinburgh :
135, Deansgate, Manchester.

Overseas :

MONTREAL (Canada) : Bible & Tract Depot, 2031, City Councillors Street.
MELBOURNE (Australia) : Keswick Book Depot, 315, Collins Street.
SYDNEY (Australia) : A. Dalrymple, 20a, Goulburn Street.
BRISBANE (Australia) : W. A. Wieland, Gospel Book Depot. Freeleagus Chambers, near Edward and Adelaide Sts.
AUCKLAND (N.Z.) : Robert Laidlaw, P.O. Box 598.
ST. LOUIS (U.S.A.) : Faithful Words Publishing Co., 1508, California Avenue.

R115/37

CONTENTS

CONTENTS—*continued*

A CERTAIN lord kept a fool, or jester, in his house, as great men did in olden times for their amusement. This lord gave a staff to his fool, and charged him to keep it until he met with a greater fool than himself, and if he met with such a one to deliver it over to him. Not many years after the lord fell sick. His fool came to see him, and was told of his master's illness. "And whither wilt thou go?" asked the fool. "On a long journey," said the lord. "And when wilt thou come again? within a month?" "No," said his master. "Within a year?" "No." "What then—never?" "Never." "And what provision hast thou made for whither thou goest?" "None at all." "Art thou going away for ever," said the fool, "and hast made no provision before thy departure? Here, take my staff, for I am not guilty of any such folly as that."

SPECIAL THROUGH CARRIAGE

ABERDEEN TO LONDON

WHILE standing one day on the platform of the Aberdeen Station, I observed a carriage with a board on it, intimating that it ran all the way from Aberdeen to London. The doors of it were open. A few individuals looked for this particular carriage, and on seeing " London " on it, they threw in their bags, entered, and seated themselves for the journey. Having furnished themselves with tickets, and satisfied themselves that they were in the right carriage, they felt the utmost confidence, nor did I observe any one of them coming out of the carriage, or running about and excitedly asking " Am I right for London ? "

Nor did I see any one refusing to enter, because the carriages provided for only a limited number by that train. There might be 80,000 inhabitants in and around Aberdeen ; but still there was not one who talked of it as absurd, for *practically* it was found to be perfectly sufficient. The carriage is for the whole city and neighbourhood, but carries only such of the inhabitants as come and seat themselves in it from day to day.

God has made provision of a similar kind. He has provided a train of grace to carry this lost world's inhabitants to heaven ; but only for as many as are willing to avail themselves of the gracious provision.

All who will may come, and, through justification by faith alone, may seat themselves in a carriage marked, "*From Guilt to Glory.*" Whenever you hear the free and general offer of salvation, you need not stand revolving the question in your own mind "Is it for me?" for just as the railway company carry ALL who comply with their printed regulations, irrespective of moral character, so if you come to the station of grace, at the advertised time, which is "*now*" (See 2 Cor. vi. 2) you will find the train of salvation ready ; and the ONLY regulation to be complied with by you, is that you consent to let the Lord Jesus Christ charge Himself with paying for your seat,—which cannot surely be anything but an easy and desirable arrangement seeing you have NO means of paying for yourself.

1st or 3rd Class

A TRAVELLER by rail can, according to his means, travel with comfort and speed by purchasing a ticket for special trains, or special classes ; and he may often have the choice of routes by which to reach his destination. But in the great journey of life it is not so ; there is no choice of class or route : only ONE WAY, only ONE PRICE ! This is made very clear and plain in God's great guide-book for life eternal. Our Lord Jesus Christ says, " I am the door : by Me if any man enter in he shall be saved." It is not one class for the rich and another class for the poor ; but Christ says to all, " I am the way." It is not one price for one and another price for another, but all are on an equality. Each sinner is redeemed ONLY with the precious blood of Christ. No silver, no gold, no works, can buy a priceless soul from perdition. Christ, alone, by virtue of His atonement for sin, can say, "I give eternal life"; "he that believeth on Me HATH everlasting life."

As the railway passenger finds the line laid, the stations built, the ticket printed, the train ready for him, and he has only to present the price named for his ticket; so in the journey to heaven, all is done for him even to the price of his ticket, which he has but to ACCEPT as a free gift from God to him, and his Salvation is perfectly secure.

My Passport to Glory

WHEN, in the darkness of the midnight train, the conductor's lamp is seen glimmering from carriage to carriage, does he hold it to your face to learn who you are, in order to be satisfied of your right to proceed? No! he lets its light fall on the ticket which you hold out to him, and if that is right, you are right, no matter who you are—rich or poor, rude or noble. So Christ, and Christ alone, is *our passport* to glory. Never can we say, Lord, look upon me, for I am holy—never; but look upon Christ, who is my passport. Unworthy? Most assuredly you are. And if you live to be outwardly the veriest saint, you will be unworthy still. God has chosen to save you. It is not a question of what you deserve, but what Christ deserves. It makes all the difference when, instead of putting our own value upon the work of Christ, and accepting it merely as meeting our need, we learn God's estimate of that work.

"It's all in the Coupling"

YOU may be a good husband, a kind father, a regular Church-goer, straight and honest ; but all this, though right in its place, is not enough. Your own good works and righteousness will never take you to heaven. Just as the furniture of the railway carriages, however rich and elegant, will never avail to move the train.

The one essential is this coupling between carriage and engine, it's all in the coupling. " Faith " is that coupling. " He that *believeth* on Me hath everlasting life." He who is united to Christ is a living soul. " He that hath not the Son of God, hath not life."

There is no power in the coupling-link itself ; its importance all comes from what it does. So, faith is a simple thing ; its only value is that it is God's plan,—by which a seeking soul is linked with a seeking Saviour ; —by which a *guilty* sinner is linked with his accepted Substitute, who died in his stead on Calvary.

It's either one thing or the other. I *have* trusted the Lord Jesus, or I've not. The coupling is either on or off. Don't say, "I hope it's on." Make sure. You may be uncertain about a good many things, but uncertainty about *salvation* is fatal. You say, "What am I to do?" Do nothing. "What am I to believe?" Believe that the Lord Jesus Christ has died in your stead, and given Himself for your sins, that you might never perish.

Though the coupling is fastened on a huge, massive hook, it might break. But Christ can *never* fail to keep the soul that trusts Him.

Though faith is necessary, it is not faith that saves, but Christ. It is not the link that pulls, but the engine. Once more, it is not a thing to which faith anchors; it is a living Person, "the Son of God who loves me, and gave Himself for me."

Can be Done while you read this

THERE must be a decision arrived at before you can become a Christian, and that can be done while you read this. You have got a question to decide for yourself, which no one can decide for you. "Are you safe for eternity ?" I may wish very much to go to Liverpool to-night to see friends who sail to-morrow: but no amount of wishing can take me to Liverpool. I must go to the station, buy a ticket, and get into the train if I am to reach that city and see my friends. And so it is with you about your soul. Wishing will not save you ; you must believe in Christ—yes, as your Saviour, and decide for Him. The responsibility rests with yourself. When Abraham's servant went to fetch a bride for his master's son from the far country, and they wished to detain him for a time, even after he had found her, he said "Hinder me not." But they thought it was too bad to send away Rebekah, never more, perhaps, to see her father and mother, and to go away with a stranger across the desert ; and so they called the damsel and put on her the responsibility, "Wilt thou go with this man ?" "And she said, I will go." Prompt decision.

Reader, "Wilt thou go with this man ?" Will you yield to the pleadings of the Holy Ghost and decide for Christ ? Why not ? You have got to do it if you would be saved.

Be like Ruth, who said, "Whither thou goest, I will go ; and where thou lodgest, I will lodge : thy people shall be my people, and thy God my God" (Ruth 1. 16, 17).

Decide now while you read this

I take Thee, Lord Jesus, to be my Saviour. Thou did'st take my place at Calvary, did'st die in my stead, as my Substitute ; and now, realizing that I have been bought with such a price, I want to live for Thee.

Halt—Right About!

"WHAT is this Conversion that you talk so much about, and say people must have ?" asked an officer one day of a private who was an earnest, active Christian.

"Sir," was the reply, "it is when the Captain of our Salvation cries '*HALT!*' and then when we halt, it is '*Right about face!*'" Conversion is more than "theory," or "head-knowledge," or "talk." It strikes deeper than the skin: it influences the heart. A reformed man is not a converted man. Conversion is not a beginning to amend or trying to be better, but is a great cure done at once, and done for ever.

An earthly doctor cures his patients by making them better every day, but conversion is God's work on man that transforms him from being a child of Satan, to being a son of God.

Conversion is a turning round, a being something that I was not before. It is having a new motive power, new hopes, desires, relationships, going a new road, sailing to another port, having a new owner, being under fresh orders.

A truly converted person will be able to say: Blind I was, now I see; Lame I was, now I walk; Dumb I was, now I speak.

Lord Jesus, make Thyself to me
A living bright reality;
More present to faith's vision keen,
Than any outward object seen;
More dear, more intimately nigh
Than e'en the sweetest earthly tie.

"Old John is dead— I am New John."

OLD John, the fish-seller of L., was a remarkable character, remarkably bad; so bad that neither God nor man could repair him; he must be made ***new***, or be useless—worse than useless—lost for ever. He was known as "drunken John, the fish-seller." One night he stumbled into a Hall where the Gospel was being preached. There he sat in bewilderment, with his bonnet on his head. Before long he was surprised to see the speaker come along to where he was sitting; and putting his hand on his shoulder, he began to speak to him kindly. John shrank back, and pushed the hand off his shoulder—not that he was displeased, but thought it was a little too much for a clean hand to touch his shoulder, which was covered with little more than black rags. But the man of God, with all the love of his Master, looked John full in the face; seeing his misery, wretchedness, and sin, his whole soul was moved with compassion for him. Putting his hand on his shoulder again, he just said, "God so loved the ***world***, that He gave His only begotten Son, that ***whosoever*** believeth in Him should not perish, but have everlasting life." The truth went right home to John's dark heart. "*God,*" he thought, "God—God so loved—the ***world***; then God must have loved poor drunken John of L——; for, drunken and guilty as I am, still I am part of the world ; there is no mistake about that."

His eyes were opened ; he saw the wide arms of God's love embracing a lost world—embracing *him*. His heart was melted, large hot tears washed white gutters down his blackened face. He saw it all; how that God had loved him, and when the broken law demanded John's life, and that John should be punished, God's Son was punished, and died in his stead. Poor old John thus received that Son, whom God had given. He was ***saved***. *For " as many as* ***received*** *Him, to them gave He power to become the sons of God, even to them that believe on His name.*"

John went away a ***new*** man. For God says, " *If any man be in Christ, he is a new creature.*" Full of joy and peace, he went to the miserable cellar he called home ! Such a home ! We need not describe it.

On entering the wretched place, his wife and only son were in. Addressing her : " Sal, lass," he said, " ***I have been converted.*** " They knew as little about conversion as he had known until that night, and so only muttered, " ***Drunk, as usual !*** " After a little time, his wife remarked that it was bed-time. " Oh ! but Sal, lass," said John, " I've been converted, and before we go to bed we must pray." " Well," thought Sal, and her son, " this is a new thing," but they at last agreed to kneel with John, if he would do the praying. Down on their knees they went, but now John was completely stumped. He never tried to pray before in his life. ***He*** knew nothing of prayer, but his heart was ***full*** with a new joy which struggled for expression. He soon remembered how he used to express his worldly joy, if ever he had any ; so taking off his Kilmarnock bonnet, he gave it a swing round his head, and shouted, " ***Hurrah for Jesus!*** " Another swing, and " Hurrah for Jesus! "—a third, and again came, " Hurrah for Jesus! "

That was all John's first prayer. It went from his overflowing heart. Jesus was beginning, middle, and end of it, and through Him it went right to the throne of God with acceptance.

The news spread abroad that John was converted, and the women of L—— gathered round him in the street, some to buy his fish, but more to see what John was like, now he was converted.

" Sure enough, there *is* a great change in him," said one. " He is not drunk," remarked another. " Not swearing as before," said a third. There was old John, with his face shining with joy, selling his fish, and telling all around, " *God so loved the world, that He gave His only begotten Son.*" He could not stop it coming from heart and tongue. Thought many, " We'll watch him and see how long this will last." But it soon became too evident, for any to doubt, that John was a *new* man.

" Father," said his son one day, " father, if you are to keep on converted, it would be as well if we could get a better house." John said little, but shortly after, seeing a nice house to let in a respectable street, he went to the landlord and said, " You have a house to let in such a street, sir." " Yes, I have ; who wants it ? " " I want it." " *You* want it ? " " Yes, I want it."

" Do you think I would let one of my respectable houses to *you* ? "

" You do not know who I am, sir."

" Oh ! yes, I know you too well."

" I think you are mistaken."

" Oh ! no, I am not mistaken, you are old drunken John, the fish-seller."

" Ah ! sir, I thought you were mistaken. *Old* John is dead. I am *new* John, ' for God so loved the world, that He gave His only begotten Son, that whosoever believeth in Him should not perish but have everlasting life.' I have believed God, and have that everlasting life." Putting his hand in his pocket, he pulled out some sovereigns, and said, " If you're afraid, sir, about your rent, I'll pay in advance." This was too much for the landlord. John's words and actions went together. He got the house, and lived in it for long, telling to all around what great things the Lord had done for his soul.

John could say, " *He loved me, and gave Himself for me.*" Won't *YOU* receive Jesus *now*, and rejoice in being *saved* ? J. M. S.

"WARRANTED TO REMOVE ALL STAINS"

AS I opened my door one morning, I found on the steps a handbill advertising a wondrous preparation for the removal of *all* stains in cloth—"sure to do it—never known to fail." I read it, and thought of other stains more foul—stains that had stuck into the textures of life, and left a sorry mark upon soul and character—guilty stains. Who is without some of these?

Oh, what effort is made to keep them out of sight—cover them up—washing "with nitre"! But the spots stick; they will not out. Much management may keep them out of others' sight, so that the garment of life is made to look tolerably respectable; but alas! they glare out, and bring discomfort and terror. One's very effort to conceal them often makes them the more prominent, —directs attention to them. Now what a sale might be made of some mixture that would "take out the stain of sin." What a market it would find! Is there anything that will do it?

Yes, a fountain, and "sinners plunged beneath that flood, lose all their guilty stains." Near? Yes, close at hand; always accessible. Costly? "Without money and without price." None so poor but may wash and be clean.—Where is it? What is it? "The blood of Jesus Christ, that cleanseth from all sin." Soul-stained, sin-defiled, will you try it?

Read what God says in Rev. 1. 5, of "Him that loved us, and washed us from our sins in His own blood."

Are You Waiting?

A YOUNG man was once awakened to cry, " What must I do to be saved ? " He went to a friend who was a professing Christian, and, unburdening his mind, eagerly and earnestly besought him to tell how salvation was to be obtained. His adviser declared that if he patiently waited, in " God's own time " he would get what he was in quest of. " But how long am I to wait ? " he asked.

" I cannot answer that question," was the reply.

Months and months passed on. He " waited," and " waited " " God's time." His agony of soul increased and grew more intense. At last he resolved to call on another friend, and seek his advice. This person told him that, instead of " waiting," he ought to pray earnestly to God for pardon, and he would obtain it.

" How long am I to pray ? " asked the anxious enquirer.

" You must just continue praying, and in due time you will receive it," was the reply.

He prayed earnestly, and besought God to give him salvation. For years he continued "striving" and "agonizing in prayer" to God, entreating Him to be reconciled, and imploring Him to "have mercy" on his soul.

At the end of three years he began to think that his friends had both given him wrong advice, and resolved to seek the counsel of another earnest Christian, and see how he had received the forgiveness of his sins. Having told what his other friends had said, and how he had been "waiting and praying," this friend pointed him to God's simple plan of salvation. He showed that all the time God had been waiting, and had been beseeching him to be reconciled, that Jesus had already taken his place, died in his stead, satisfied the law and paid his debt. The mistake discovered, he immediately "took God at His word." God says: "Come unto Me all ye that labour and are heavy laden, and I will give you rest."

The Settled Account

"IS that account settled?" "Yes, sir, it is; here is the receipt for it." "Then put it away on the file; it is done with." So it was filed and put away.

As man does with his earthly accounts, so God does with His heavenly accounts. We, His creatures, owed Him a large debt; Jesus Christ, the sinner's Substitute, paid the debt for us; it therefore has become a settled account; the receipt in full is before God in the person of His Son. Can any receipt for our debt, any discharge, be more full, and complete, than these words?—

> "He * * having forgiven you all trespasses, blotting out the handwriting of ordinances that was against us * * took it out of the way, nailing it to His Cross."
> —Col. 2. 14.

If a man makes application for an account that has been previously paid, he is only satisfied upon our producing the receipt. Now, if you won't believe that your debt has been paid, and won't produce the receipt—the law holds you as a debtor to pay the whole. You will be pressed to pay that great debt that you owe. Jesus Christ has provided for it; but if you won't believe it and so produce the receipt, think of the awful consequence.

Why are Men put into Gaol?

NOT because of a life of wickedness, but for some one wrong act or deed. They broke the law once, and perhaps only for a few minutes; but for that they have to suffer for months or years afterwards. No one considers it a violation of justice so to punish.

Men are punished by God, not because they have led a wicked life, but for one sin—UNBELIEF—in Christ. "He that believeth on Him is not condemned, but he that believeth not, is condemned already."

God does not say, he that liveth a good life here shall have eternal life hereafter; but He plainly shows that a person's safety or ruin turns on the acceptance or rejection of Christ Jesus, the sacrifice and atonement that He has made.

It necessarily follows, however, that he who accepts Christ has to obey Christ. Faith in Christ is proved by works for Christ. Where there is a live root we expect fruit. He who says "I believe," and yet lives in sin, is "a liar, and the truth is not in him."

"Know ye not, that to whom ye yield yourselves servants to obey, his servants ye are to whom ye obey; whether of sin unto death, or of obedience unto righteousness?" (Romans 6. 16.)

Captain John Couts

HE was a wild, swearing tyrant of a sea captain, but on one voyage he was taken ill and lay on his back in mid-ocean, death staring him in the face. He winced in the presence of death, and fear of "the beyond" took fast hold upon him. At last he sent for the first officer and said, "Williams, get on your knees and pray a bit for a fellow; I'm awful bad; expect I'll go this time." "I'm not a praying man, captain; can't pray." "Well, bring your Bible and read me a bit—for my rope's about run out." "I've no Bible, captain." "Well, then, send the second officer here, perhaps he can pray a bit." The second officer then stood by his bunk. "Say,—Thomas, I'm afraid I'm bound for eternity this trip; get down and pray, if you can." "I'd do it, captain,—if I could," said the second officer, "but since I was a lad I've never prayed." "Have you a Bible, then?" said the captain. "No, sir." "Then tell the third officer I want to see him," said the captain. The third officer was like his superiors; neither could pray, or had a Bible.

Alas, for the dying captain! They searched the ship for a man that prayed, or had a Bible. At last one of the men came and said he had seen a book like the Bible in the hands of the cook's boy, Willie Platt. " Just see if he has one," —said the captain. " Sonny, have you got a Bible ? " " Yes," said the boy, " but I only read it in my own time." " Oh, that's all right, boy. Fetch it and sit down here and find out something that will help me. I'm going to die. Find something about God having mercy on sinners." Poor boy! he didn't know where to read ; but remembered his mother had oft made him read the 53rd chapter of Isaiah. Willie turned to that chapter and read. When he got to the 5th verse, " He was wounded for our transgressions, He was bruised for our iniquities : the chastisement of our peace was upon Him ; and with His stripes are we healed," the captain, who had been listening for his life and, realizing that he was certainly having his last chance, said,—" Stop, boy, now that sounds like it ; read it again." Once more Willie read those words, " He was wounded for our transgressions, He was bruised for our iniquities : the chastisement of our peace was upon Him ; and with His stripes are we healed." " Aye, boy, that's good, that's it." Willie then got braver, and said, " Captain, when I was reading that verse at home, mother made me

put my name in it; may I put it in now just where mother told me?" "Certainly, sonny, go on, put your name in just where she told you." Reverently the boy read, "He was wounded for Willie Platt's transgressions, He was bruised for Willie Platt's iniquities: the chastisement of Willie Platt's peace was upon Him; and with His stripes Willie Platt is healed." By then, as Willie finished, the captain was half over his bedside, and eagerly said, "Boy, read again and put your captain's name in,—John Couts, John Couts." Then the boy read—"He was wounded for John Couts' transgressions, He was bruised for John Couts' iniquities; the chastisement of John Couts' peace was upon Him; and with His stripes John Couts is healed." When He had finished the captain said, "That'll do, boy, go on deck."—Then he lay back—having heard those glorious words ringing in his ears—he over and over repeated them, putting his own name in,—and as he did so, the joys of heaven filled the heart of a new-born soul. Another poor sinner for whom Christ died had now believed Him and received Him (John 1. 12).—**Yes, it says, "as many as received Him, TO THEM gave He the power to become the sons of God." A few days after the soul of the captain passed away,—the**

body was rolled in canvas, and over the ship's side disappeared into the ocean, there to remain till Jesus comes, and the sea gives up its dead (See John v. 28, 29). **But, before his spirit took its flight, John Couts had witnessed *to every man aboard his ship,*—that Jesus was wounded for *his* transgressions,—was bruised for *his* iniquities, and by His stripes, he, John Couts, was healed.**

God commended His love even toward that wild swearing sea captain, and He alike loves us; God says: "He was wounded for *our* transgressions."

Have you "put *your* name in" yet?

O, Saviour, I have naught to plead
In heaven above or earth beneath,
Save Thine exceeding love and my exceeding need.
The need will soon be past and gone,
Exceeding great but quickly o'er;
The love, unbought, is all Thine own,
And lasts for evermore.

"NOT FOR ME"

"WITHOUT money, and without price!" Such are the terms on which God offers to all the gift of eternal life. Wonderful message of love! yet more wonderful how few will take it on these terms. An incident which happened a short time ago will illustrate my meaning.

A friend of the poor was often known to order a quarter of a ton of coals to be taken to persons whom he knew to be in distress. The weather was severe one winter, the snow lying thick, and the kind donor rejoiced to think what warmth and comfort his gifts would bring to many hearts and homes. The coal cart drew up opposite a poor desolate-looking cottage, and the coalman knocked at the door, and told the old man within that he had brought him some coals. "Who from?" "Don't know," says the man, "but I was told to bring 'em here, and here they are."

"It's a mistake; they're not for me," answered the old man. "No such luck for me—I've no friend to send me coals for nothing." "Nay, but they're for the man as lives at the dyke. Ain't that you?"

"That's me, sure enough; but there's a mistake; it's some other dyke, maybe."

"Nonsense, man; take 'em, and be thankful. I can't stay here all day talking."

"Take 'em away then: they're not for me, and I won't have anything to do with 'em." And he shut the door, and returned to his desolate hearth. The cart rolled away, taking in it the gift that was intended for the old man.

The next day the same cart was seen drawn up opposite a low court in the town, and the same man, with a quarter of a ton of coals, knocking at one of the doors. "I've brought you some coals," he says cheerfully; "where shall I put 'em?"

"They're not for me," answered the man who opened the door; "it's a mistake."

"It's no mistake," says the coalman. "See, here's the order:—No. 24, quarter of a ton of coals. Now, that's clear, ain't it?"

"That's my number, certainly," replied the other; "but these coals ain't mine, and I can't take 'em in. They must be for some one else!"

"Well," says the man with the coals, scratching his head with a puzzled look, "these coals beat me; they're more trouble than enough. One would think I was bringing yer poison. Here comes a nice present of coals, and yer clean refuse to take 'em. But leave 'em I shall; for yesterday I took 'em away from a house, and got into trouble for it. So, if yer don't open yer cellar door, I shall chuck 'em down here by yer doorstep."

Thus pressed, the man at last opened his cellar door, saying, "You'll soon be back to fetch 'em, I guess, so I won't set too much store by 'em. But if they're for me, I'm sure I'm much obliged."

One more house the coalman visits with

his load, and, knocking at the door, tells the woman he has brought her some coals.

"For me?" she says; "oh, it can't be true; they must be for someone else."

"No, mum, here's your number, plain enough:—No. 8, quarter of a ton of coals."

"So it is! Well, then, I suppose God has sent 'em to me, for no one else knows that the last bit of coal is on the fire now. Bring them in. I must thank Him."

"Perhaps you'd better," is the man's short answer; but to himself he adds, "She's the only sensible one; the rest are fools."

Yes. How many such fools there are in the world! Even though "God so loved the world, that He gave His only begotten Son, that *whosoever* believeth in Him should not perish, but have everlasting life" (John 3. 16). "The gift of God" (Romans 6. 23).

The coals were paid for by the donor: so our salvation has been bought with a price, even the precious blood of the Son of God, "Who gave Himself a ransom for all" (1 Timothy 2. 6).

Yet, though God offers to each one the *free gift* of eternal life, we act like these cottagers and the coals. Some, like the old man, refuse it altogether. "It's not for me."

"Herein is love, not that we loved God, but that He loved us and sent His Son to be the propitiation for our sins" (1 John 4. 10).

"Such an Offer"

"SUCH an offer!" Full and free!
Is it really meant for me?
That all my sins on Christ were laid,
That all my debt by Him was paid?
Yes; Jesus says it, who has died:—
"Believe," and thou art justified.

Such an offer! Pardon now
For hidden sin, and broken vow!
For years of cold neglect and scorn;
Can mercy's ray upon me dawn?
Yes: Jesus died instead of thee;
His death for thine, must be thy plea.

Such an offer! Peace and joy
Untainted by the world's alloy;
The sweet assurance of a Friend
Who, loving, loves unto the end;
The knowledge now of sins forgiven
And of a Home prepared in heaven.

Oh, what goodness!—Lord, I take
This offer Thou dost freely make!
My one desire shall henceforth be
To live for Him who died for me.
Spread glad news, thro' every nation!
Instant—free—and full salvation.

AN only daughter of wealthy and worldly parents in America, when once absent from home, was brought to hear of, and to accept Christ as her Saviour. With joy she returned to tell her parents, but in their displeasure they alternately reproached and pleaded with her to give up her new found riches; finally,—her father threatening her with loss of home and inheritance, asked her *decision.*—With tearful eyes, and aching heart, she listened; and then drawing up to her piano, with beautiful voice she sang out her reply—in the above words. Later by her testimony both parents were brought to Christ.

"Fire if You Dare!"

WE do not remember a more striking illustration of the sheltering value of the Saviour's blood than the following incident, which occurred some few years ago :—

In one of the Spanish-speaking towns in South America, a British subject was arrested for joining in some local riot. He was condemned to be shot, and brought out before a file of soldiers for that purpose. Without avail the British and American consuls protested against the act. Suddenly, just as the officer was about to give the word FIRE ! the British consul rushed to the side of the condemned man, wrapped him in the British "Union Jack," and cried, "Fire if you dare!" The American consul also wrapped around him the "Stars and Stripes," and stood on the other side. The result was that the arms were grounded, and the man delivered over to the British protection.

The sinner who believes in Jesus is saved by being covered with the robe of Christ's righteousness; for there is "no condemnation to them which are in Christ Jesus." He is redeemed with the precious blood of Christ, and protected as one of God's children.

OH, the peace my Saviour gives,
Peace I never knew before;
And my way has brighter grown,
Since I've learn'd to trust Him more.

I Don't Hope at All

ONE day, at the seaside, as I walked with a respectable and religious farmer, we met a fisherman, to whom I spoke, asking if his sins were forgiven.

"No, they're not," was the straightforward reply. "Oh, but I *hope* we're all forgiven," said the farmer.

"But I don't *hope* at all," I continued. "I'm sure about *mine.* Though, like you, only a poor unworthy sinner, I trust to Jesus, as having paid my debt when He died on the cross. He says, 'He that believeth hath everlasting life,' and I just take Him at His word. Now let me make this plain. If a gentleman were to buy a boat, and give it to our friend here, and he accepted it, and took possession of it, he would not say that he *hoped* to have a new boat, but that he was *sure he had one.* Now I hope to enjoy heaven, because I am not there yet; but I do not *hope* to be forgiven, when God tells me plainly that He has blotted out my sins."

"I have blotted out, as a thick cloud, thy transgressions, and, as a cloud, thy sins: return unto Me for I have redeemed thee" (Isa. 44. 22).

Only Two Classes

THERE were two classes in the day of Noah's flood, those who were inside the ark, and those who were outside; two in the parable of the gospel-net, the good fish and the bad; two in the parable of the ten virgins, the wise and the foolish; two in the account of the judgment-day, the sheep and the goats; two sides of the throne, the right hand and the left; two, only two abodes, when the last sentence is passed, only heaven and hell.

TOO CHEAP

A PREACHER of the Gospel had gone down into a coal mine, during the noon hour, to tell the miners of that grace and truth which came by Jesus Christ. After telling them the simple story of God's love to lost sinners, —man's state, and God's remedy—a full and free salvation offered,—the time came for the men to resume work, and the preacher came back to the shaft, to ascend to the world again. Meeting the foreman, he asked him what he thought of God's way of salvation ? The man replied :

" Oh, it is too cheap ; I cannot believe in such a religion as that ! "

Without an immediate answer to his remark, the preacher asked : " How do you get out of this place ? "

" Simply by getting into the cage," was the reply. " And does it take long to get to the top ? "

" Oh, no ; only a few seconds ! "

" Well, that certainly is very easy and simple. But do you not need to help raise yourself ? " said the preacher.

" Of course not ! " replied the miner. " As I have said, you have nothing to do but get into the cage."

" But what about the people who sunk the shaft, and perfected all this arrangement; was there much labour, care, thought, and expense about it ?"

"Indeed, yes; that was a laborious and expensive work. The shaft is eighteen hundred feet deep, and it was sunk at great cost to the proprietor; but it is our only way out, and without it we should never be able to get to the surface."

"Just so. And when God's word tells you that whosoever believeth on the Son of God hath everlasting life, you at once say, 'Too cheap!'—'Too cheap!' forgetting that God's work to bring you and others out of the pit of destruction and death, ***was accomplished at a vast cost, the price being the death of His Son."***

Men talk about the "help of Christ" in their salvation—that if they do their part, Christ will do His; forgetting that the Lord Jesus Christ by Himself purged our sins, and that their part is but to accept what has been done.

My Individual Saviour

My salvation depends upon my taking Christ as my individual Saviour, just as if He had died **for me alone**: with David I claim the "good Shepherd" as "my own individual Shepherd." As St. Paul says, "safely hid with Christ."

IT IS SO DARK

THERE come seasons of darkness in all our lives—times when there is neither sun, nor moon, nor stars in the sky, and we stand still in fear, or grope, trembling.

A few years ago there fell upon my life one of these seasons, in which I could see neither to the right nor the left. A terror of darkness was upon me.

One night I lay awake, thinking, thinking, until my brain grew wild with uncertainty. I could not see a step in advance, and feared to move onward, lest with the next footfall I should plunge into hopeless ruin. Very strongly was I tempted to turn aside from the way in which I was going—a way reason and conscience approved as right: but something held me back. Again and again I took up and considered the difficulties of my situation, looking to the right hand and the left for ways of extrication; inclining now to go in this direction, and now in that; yet always held away from resolve by inner convictions of right and duty, that grew clear at the moment when

I was ready to give up my hold on integrity. So the hours went, heavy-footed, until past midnight. My little daughter was sleeping in the crib beside my bed. But now she began to move uneasily, and presently her timid voice broke faintly :—

"Papa!" she called.

"What is it, darling?" I asked.

"O papa, it is dark! Take Nellie's hand!" I reached out my hand and took her tiny one in my own, clasping it firmly. A sigh of relief came up from her little heart. All her loneliness and fear were gone, and in a few moments she was sound asleep again.

"O my Father in heaven!" I cried, in a sudden, almost wild, outburst of feeling. "It is dark, very dark. Take my hand!"

A great peace fell upon me. The terror of darkness was gone. "Keep hold of my hand, O my Father!" I prayed fervently; "and though I should be called to walk through the valley and the shadow of death, I will fear no evil. Let not my feet wander to the right nor to the left."

CHRIST ALONE

JESUS has done all that God deemed necessary to be done to ensure complete pardon, acceptance, and salvation to all who believe in His name. If you take Jesus as your Saviour, you build securely for eternity, for God says, " other foundation can no man lay than that is laid, which is Jesus Christ." He is the foundation stone of salvation laid by God Himself, and on His finished atoning work alone, you are instructed to rest the salvation of your soul, not on anything accomplished by you, wrought in you, felt by you, or proceeding from you. Christ without you, and not the work of the Spirit within you, that must form the **sole** ground of your deliverance from guilt. Beware of resting your peace on your feelings, tears, repentance, prayers, duties, or resolutions. *Begin* with receiving Christ. He must be *everything* **or He will be nothing.**

O CHRIST, what burdens bowed Thy head!
Our load was laid on Thee;
Thou stoodest in the sinner's stead,
Didst bear all ill for me.
A Victim led, Thy blood was shed,
Now, there's no load for me.

Death and the curse were in our cup:
O Christ, 'twas full for Thee!
But Thou hast drained the last dark drop,
'Tis empty now for me:
That bitter cup, love drank it up,
NOW, blessing's draught for me.

Jehovah lifted up his rod;
O Christ, it fell on Thee!
Thou wast sore stricken of Thy God;
There's not one stroke for me.
Thy tears, Thy blood, beneath it flowed;
Thy bruising healeth me.

For me, Lord Jesus, Thou hast died,
And I have died in Thee:
Thou'rt ris'n—my bands are all untied;
And now Thou liv'st in me;
When purified, made white, and tried,
Thy Glory then for me.

"I CAN GO IN WITH THEM"

I HAVE read, said Mr. Spurgeon, of one who dreamed a dream, when in great distress of mind, about religion. He thought he stood in the outer court of heaven, and he saw a glorious host marching up, singing sweet hymns, and bearing the banners of victory. They passed by him through the gate, and he heard in the distance sweet strains of music.

"Who are they ?" he asked.

"They are the goodly fellowship of the Prophets, who have gone to be with God."

He heaved a deep sigh as he said, "Alas ! I am not one of them, and never shall be, and I cannot enter there."

By and by there came another band, equally lovely in appearance, and equally triumphant, robed in white. They passed within the portals, and again were shouts of welcome heard.

"Who are they ?"

"They are the goodly fellowship of the Apostles."

"Alas !" he said, "I belong not to that fellowship, and I cannot enter there."

He still waited and lingered, in the hope that he might yet go in; but the next multitude did not encourage him, for they were the noble army of Martyrs. He could not go with them, nor wave their palm branches. He waited still, and saw that the next was a company of godly ministers and officers of Christian Churches; but he could not go with them.

At last, as he walked, he saw a larger host than all the rest put together, marching and singing most melodiously, and in front walked the woman that was a sinner, and the thief that died upon the cross. He looked long, and saw there Manasseh, and the like; and, when they entered, he could see who they were, and he thought, "There will be no shouting about them." But, to his astonishment, it seemed as if all heaven was rent with sevenfold shouts as they passed in. And the angels said to him, "These are they that are mighty sinners, saved by mighty grace."

And then he said, "Blessed be God! *I can go in with them.*"

And so he awoke.

"I am that Clown"

IT is simply a delusion to think that because you see persons laughing and indulging in noisy merriment, they must necessarily be happy ! A loud laugh or empty joke is often one of the coverings to conceal an aching heart.

A man once went to consult a doctor about his health : he complained that he suffered from such overwhelming depression that his life was unbearable. The doctor examined him, and after a little remarked that he wanted nothing except some lively amusement, to divert his thoughts from himself. "Try a good novel—that would be about the best medicine you could take." The man shook his head, as if doubtful of the prescription, and then the doctor said again, "Well, I'll tell you what to do to cheer yourself up ; go to such and such a theatre, and see what that will do for you." Still a turn of the head showed the patient had no confidence in the proposal helping him. "Well," said the doctor, "I can but think of one other thing or person that would help you, and if that does not do so, I am unable to help you. Go and see that great clown that has lately arrived, and is drawing such crowds with his merriment; and if you suffer from depression after hearing and watching him, I shall be surprised."

"Ah!" said the poor man at once, in a tone of the deepest distress, **"I am that Clown."**

There are many who might tell the same tale. Jesus says, "Come unto ME, all ye that labour and are heavy laden, and I will give you rest"—REST dearly purchased for you. The Lord Jesus left His throne above, and came down here, that He might buy it for you. He now offers it freely to you.

"Herrings for Nothing"

I WANT you to think of a bitter east windy day, fast falling snow, and a short, muddy street in London. Put these thoughts together, and add to them the picture of a tall stout man, in a rough coat, and with a large comforter round his neck, buffeting through wind and storm. The darkness is coming rapidly, as a man with a basket on his head turns the corner of the street, and there are two of us on opposite sides. He cries loudly as he goes: "Herrings! three a penny! Red herrings, good and cheap, three a penny!" So crying, he passes along the street, crosses at its end, and comes back to where I am standing at the corner. Here he pauses, evidently wishing to fraternize with somebody, as a relief from disappointed hopes of trade. I presume I appear a suitable object, as he commences conversation:—

"Governor, what do you think of these 'ere herrings?"—three in his hand, while the remaining stock are deftly balanced in the basket on his head. "Don't you think they're good?" and he offered me the opportunity of testing them by scent, which I courteously but firmly declined, "and don't you think they're cheap as well?"

I asserted my decided opinion that they were good and cheap.

"Then, look here, governor, why can't I sell 'em? Yer have I walked a mile and a half along this dismal place, offering these good and cheap uns; and nobody don't buy none!"

"I do not wonder at all at that," I answered, to his astonishment.

"Tell us why not, governor."

"The people have no work, and are starving; there are plenty of houses round here that have not a single penny in them," was my reply.

"Ah! then, governor," he rejoined, "I've put my foot in it this time; I knew they was werry poor, but I thought three a penny 'ud tempt 'em. But if they haven't the ha'pence, they can't spend 'em, sure enough: so there's nothing for it but to carry 'em back, and try and sell 'em elsewhere. I thought by selling cheap, arter buying cheap, I could do them good, and earn a trifle for myself. But I'm done this time."

"How much will you take for the lot?" I inquired.

First a keen look at me—then down came the basket from his head—then a rapid calculation—then a grinning inquiry,—"Do you mean profit an' all, governor?"—"Yes."

"Then I'll take four shillin', and be glad to get 'em."

I put my hand in my pocket, produced that amount, and handed it to him.

"Right! governor, thank'ee! Now what'll I do with 'em?" he said, as he quickly transferred the coins to his own pocket.

" Go round this corner into the middle of the road, and shout with all your might: '*Herrings for nothing*!' and give three to every man, woman, or child that comes to you, till the basket is emptied."

On hearing these instructions, he immediately reproduced the money, and examined it. Being satisfied of its genuineness, he again replaced it, and then looked keenly and questioningly at me.

" Well," I said, " is it all right and good ? "

" Yes," replied he.

" Then the herrings are my property, and I can do as I like with them ; but if you don't like to do as I tell you, give me my money back."

" All right ! governor, an' they *are* yours ; so if you says it, here goes ! " Accordingly he proceeded into the middle of the adjoining street, and went along, shouting aloud : " Herrings for nothing ! good red herrings for nothing ! "

Out of sight myself, I stood at the corner to watch his progress ; and speedily he neared the house where a tall woman stood at the first floor window, looking out upon him.

" Here you are, missus," he bawled, " herrings for nothing ! a fine chance for yer ; come an' take 'em ! "

The woman shook her head unbelievingly, and left the window.

" Vot a fool ! " said he ; " but they won't

be all so. Herrings for nothing!" A little child came out to look at him, and he called to her, "Yer, my dear, take these in to your mother, tell her how cheap they are—herrings for nothing." But the child was afraid of him, and them, and ran indoors. So down the street, in the snowy slush and mud, went the cheap fish, the vendor crying loudly as he went, "Herrings for nothing!" and then adding savagely, "Oh, you fools!" Thus he reached the very end; and, turning to retrace his steps, he continued his double cry as he came, "Herrings for nothing!" and then, in a lower key, "Oh, you fools!"

"Well!" I said to him calmly, as he reached me at the corner.

"Well!" he replied, "*if* yer think so! When you gave me the money for herrings as yer didn't want, I thought you was training for a lunatic asylum! Now I thinks all the people round here are fit company for yer. But what'll I do with the herrings, if yer don't want 'em and they won't have 'em?"

"We'll try again, together," I replied; "I'll come with you, and we'll both shout."

Into the road we both went; and he shouted: "Herrings for nothing!" and then I called out also, "Will any one have some herrings for tea?"

They heard the voice, knew it; and they came out, in twos and threes and sixes, men and women and children; all striving eagerly to reach the welcome food.

As fast as I could take them from the basket, I handed three to each eager applicant, until all were speedily disposed of. When the basket was empty, the hungry crowd who had none, was far greater than those that had been supplied; but they were too late; there were no more herrings.

Foremost amongst the disappointed was the tall woman, who, with a bitter tongue, began vehemently, "Why haven't I got any? Ain't I as good as they? Ain't my children as hungry as theirs?"

Before I had time to reply, the vendor stretched out his arm towards her, saying: "Why, governor, that's the very woman as I offered 'em to first, and she turned up her nose."

"I didn't," she rejoined passionately; "I didn't believe you meant it!"

"Yer just goes without, then, for yer unbelief!" he replied. "Good night, and thank-'ee, governor!"

You smile at the story, which is strictly true. Are you sure you are not ten thousand times worse? Their unbelief only cost them a hungry stomach; but what may your unbelief of God's offer cost you? God—not man—GOD has sent His messenger to you repeatedly for years, to offer pardon *for nothing!* Salvation *for nothing!* and what have you replied? Have *you* not turned away in scornful unbelief, like the woman?

God says:—"Because I have called, and ye

refused; I have stretched out My hand, and no man regarded: I also will laugh at your calamity; I will mock when your fear cometh" (Prov. 1. 24, 26). But God also says:—

"Ho, every one that thirsteth, come ye to the waters, and he that hath no money; come ye, buy, and eat; yea, come, buy wine and milk without money and without price" (Isa. 55. 1).—"For God so loved the world, that He gave His only begotten Son, that whosoever believeth in Him should not perish, but have everlasting life" (John 3. 16).

Answer Him. Will you have it?

Wonderful Grace!

Wonderful Mercy!

Wonderful Wisdom!

God so loves each one of us, that He has sent His own Son to be the Sacrifice for our sins, that whoever will accept Him may be at once pardoned and have eternal life; and more than that, He gives to all who do accept Him—present joy, peace, happiness, guidance, help for every day and hour we live down here.

Forgot His Broom

SOME years ago, there was a crossing-sweeper in Dublin, with his broom, at the corner. His highest thoughts were to keep the crossing clean, and look for the pence. One day a lawyer who knew him put his hand upon his shoulder, and said : " My good fellow, do you know that you are heir to a fortune of so many pounds a year ? " (naming the sum).

" Do you mean it ? " asked the crossing-sweeper.

" I do," replied the lawyer. " I have just received the information. I am sure that you are the man."

The man was convinced. He left his crossing, and at once walked away. Forgetting his broom, he made haste to know all about his inheritance, like the woman of Samaria, who " left her water-pot " by Jacob's well, and hastened to the city to proclaim the presence of the Messiah whom she had seen.

How many of us talk of our title to a heavenly and eternal heritage, and yet hold fast the broom, and cling to all the cares and coppers of this world ? Oh, man, look up ! It is often too evident we don't really believe it.

A Moment of Time

IT is in a moment that the most solemn of all decisions is made—the soul's surrender to the Lord Jesus Christ. The soul itself, amidst the conflict of emotion, may scarce be able to tell the precise moment when the 'Yes' is spoken; or it may lie back in the dim child-time, and be forgotten. There may have been long preparation going forward, and the soul may have been hesitating and trembling as on the verge of surrender: but the 'Yes' that means acceptance of Christ and His salvation is spoken in a moment.

A moment may make the difference between life and death. Too late may be too late by a moment only. The missing of the right moment may be the missing of the "accepted time."

HOW SHALL WE ESCAPE IF WE NEGLECT SO GREAT SALVATION?

"IS FATHER ON DECK?"

YEARS ago, Captain D—— commanded a vessel sailing from Liverpool to New York, and on one voyage he had all his family with him on board. One night, when all were asleep, there arose a sudden squall, which came sweeping over the waters until it struck the vessel, and threw her almost on her side, tumbling and crashing everything that was movable, and awakening the passengers to a consciousness that they were in imminent peril.

Every one on board was alarmed; and some sprang from their berths and began to dress.

Captain D—— had a little girl on board, just eight years old, who of course awoke with the rest.

"What's the matter?" cried the frightened child.

They told her a squall had struck the ship.

"Is father on deck?" said she.

"Yes, father's on deck."

The little thing dropped herself on her pillow again without a fear, and in a few moments was fast asleep, in spite of winds or waves.

Child of God, shame to your doubts and fears,—is not our Father on deck? Remember this when the next squall strikes your barque: "I will never leave thee, nor forsake thee."

"A Thousand Guineas if You'll take me in"

WHEN the steamer *London*, which was bound for Melbourne with some hundreds of passengers on board, foundered in the Bay of Biscay, a thrilling tale was told by the few survivors, of a lady who offered a thousand guineas to be saved. The great steamship was fast settling down amidst the heavy seas, and all hope was given up except for those in the only boat that was safely launched. The lady had refused to get into the boat when she had a chance, but after it had got but a very little way from the side of the sinking steamer, seeing that she must go down with all the rest on board, with a face livid with horror, she piteously cried out, "A thousand guineas if you'll take me in." But money—even millions—were then valueless. It was too late—she was lost, through rejecting the offer.

Saved in Three Minutes

By Dr. A. J. GORDON.

COMING out of Church not long since, a messenger met me, requesting that I would go at once to see a young man who was near his end.

I went at once, and on entering the room sat down by the bed; and seeing the time was short, I came at once to the all-important subject, and said:

"Friend, I see that you are very ill,—are you prepared for what is before you?" —"Wish I only were," he replied, giving me a look of despair. "If I could but be spared for two or three weeks I believe I might be prepared,—but, the Doctor tells me, I cannot live but for only a few hours probably." So saying he caught hold of my hand, and held it as a drowning man would hold on to a plank.

"Three weeks," I said,—"Why do you want three weeks?"—Then he went on to give me his idea of preparation and conversion. "You see," he said, "there must first be conviction;—***then,*** time for a careful review of my life,—and its sins. And ***then,*** there must be repentance, and Godly sorrow, long and deep, to be acceptable to God. And ***then*** Faith, and the new birth,—***when*** the heart by this process has been made ready. All of which must occupy some weeks." Having given me this detailed account of "The Plan of Salvation,"—he sank back exhausted,—and looked imploringly as if to say, "You see that you can do nothing for me, it's too late."

"What!" I exclaimed. "Three weeks in order to be saved? Let me tell you that you may be saved,—yes, in ***three minutes***," —and so saying I opened the Word of God, and read,—"As many as receive Him, to them He gave power to become the sons of God,—even to them that believe on His Name."—"If I give you this gold watch," I asked, "how long would it take you to receive it? Could you not take it ***at once***?" —He assented.

"The gift of God is Eternal Life," I said. "What have you to do with a gift? Do you buy it or beg it, or wait a long time to be prepared to accept it?—God offers His Son to you, and Eternal Life,—and says 'He that hath the Son hath life, and he that hath not the Son, hath not life.'—In order to have a gift you have to take it, and in order to have the Son of God, you must just take Him."

With an earnest look he replied, "But how can I take Him? Do tell me exactly the way to do it," he pleaded. Turning to Romans 10. I said, "Here you have the way told you ***exactly***:—'If thou shalt confess with thy mouth the Lord Jesus, and shalt believe in thine heart that God has raised Him from the dead, thou shalt be saved.'" —"Now," I said, "if you want to be saved just accept Jesus as your Saviour,—and tell Him that you do so."—So saying I knelt by his side, and asked him to follow me in a simple prayer of acceptance.—"Lord Jesus, I come to Thee. I am a sinner, Thou art the ***Saviour***. I take Thee now to be my Saviour. I trust Thee,—receive

**Thee, and I put my soul in Thy hands."—
That was all.**

Then I went away to attend other duties, but felt confident that an acceptance of saving faith had been exercised.—Some hours later in the evening I called again, and was shown into the same room, where the conversation had taken place.—There lay the young man, in the sleep of death, with the calm of Heaven on his face.—" Oh,"—said the leader or lady of the household,—" if you *could* have heard him talk to us some time after you went away;—he called us all in, and said, ' Isn't it wonderful, that minister showed me how I could be saved, yes, in three minutes,—when I had been thinking I must have weeks to prepare to die,' and he added, ' Oh, come and kneel down here. I want to *thank* and praise God, that He has saved me,' " and the lady added, " Such a triumphant death I have never witnessed."

Some people object to the term " instantaneous conversion," but we assert from Scripture that one may be without Eternal Life at one moment, and then, upon realizing and accepting the finished work of Christ, possess it the next moment. " He that believeth on the Son hath Eternal Life."—Yes, and at the same moment as when he believes.—Blessed be God that He can save you, reader, in " Three Minutes," yes, even "In One Minute," *when* you simply believe, and thank Him, that He " loved *you*,—and gave Himself for *you*."

Let your Bucket Down

THE great river Amazon pours out so mighty a stream of fresh water into the Atlantic, that for miles out of sight of land, just opposite the mouth of the river, the water in the ocean is entirely fresh.

Some years ago a sailing ship left Europe for a South American port, and, through storm and mishap, was so long on its voyage that the water on board began to give out; and, though the crew took every care, they shortly found themselves with their last tank or last cask empty.

A day or two later, though becalmed in a hot climate, to their great joy and relief they sighted another vessel, and, when near enough to signal, they ran up their flags, telling of their piteous position: "We're dying for want of water."

To their astonishment, the reply that came back quickly, seemed almost to mock them: "Water all around you; let your bucket down."

Little did they know that they were just then crossing the mighty Amazon's ocean current, and, instead of being in salt water, they were actually sailing in fresh. Water all around them, though out of sight of land!

Fellow-traveller, you may be crying out, "What must I do to be saved?" little realizing that the ocean of God's love is **all around you. "Let your bucket down!"**

"Are You a Sceptic?"

IT is told of a celebrated infidel lecturer, how, after he had concluded one of his lectures in a village, he challenged those present to discussion. Who should accept the challenge but an old, bent woman, who went up to the lecturer, and said :— "Sir, I have a question to put to you."

"Well, my good woman, what is it?"

"Ten years ago," she said, "I was left a widow, with eight children utterly unprovided for, and nothing to call my own but this Bible. By its direction, and looking to God for strength, I have been enabled to feed myself and family. I am now tottering to the grave, but perfectly happy, because I look forward to a life of immortality with Jesus in heaven. What has **your** way of thinking done for you?"

"Well, my good lady," rejoined

the lecturer, "I don't want to disturb your comfort ; but——"

"Oh ! that's not the question," interposed the woman ; "keep to the point, sir. What has your way of thinking done for you ?"

The infidel endeavoured to shirk the matter again ; but the feeling of the meeting gave vent to applause, and the infidel had to go, discomfited.

The mother of Hume, the infidel philosopher, was once a professor of Christianity. Dazzled by the genius of her son, she followed him into the mazes of scepticism. Years passed and she drew near the gates of death, and from her dying bed she wrote :

"My dear son,—My health has failed me. I am in a deep decline. I cannot live long. Your philosophy affords me no comfort in my distress. I am left without hope or consolation, and my mind is sinking into a state of despair. I pray you, hasten home to console me, or, at least, write to me the consolations that *philosophy* affords at this dying hour."

Men may *live* without Christ, but they cannot *die* without Christ. You may scoff at the words "Heaven" and "Hell," but they are **solemn realities.**

Why be wise for time, but a fool for eternity? What may horrify you is, that my life has been saved by the death of another, in my stead, and that God should have **so** loved me as to give His own Son to torture and death for me. But this is **God's plan.**

If you reject so great Salvation, there remains nothing for you but fearful judgment. Remorse, anguish, despair! why, these words don't half describe what it will be "where hope will never come!"

But why should you ever come to this, when the Son of God, *who loved you and gave Himself for you,* is even now beseeching you to believe that HE has died in your stead, to see the Son of God as **your** substitute, and to lay hold on eternal life.

Learning to Float

THERE is a story told of a young man, who was seeking after the knowledge of eternal security and peace with God.

The friend to whom he had confided his difficulties, discerned very quickly that he was striving to attain everlasting life by his own efforts. He spoke of " sincere prayers " and " heartfelt desires " after salvation, but continually lamented that he did not feel " any different in spite of it all."

His friend did not answer him at first, but presently he interrupted him with the inquiry, " W——, did you ever learn to float ? "

" Yes, I did ! " was the surprised reply.

" And did you find it easy to learn ? "

" Not at first ! " he answered.

" What was the difficulty ? Tell me."

" Well, the fact was, I could not lie still ; I could not believe or realize that the water could hold me up, without any effort of my own ; so I always began to struggle, and of course down I went at once." " And then ? "

" Why, then I found out that I must only just rest, *give up all the struggle,* and the water would bear me up. It was easy enough after that ; I was able to lie back in the fullest confidence that I should never sink."

" And is not God's Word more worthy of your trust than the changeable sea ? He does not bid you wait for feelings. He commands you just to rest in Him, to believe His Word and accept His gift. His message of life reaches down to you in your place of ruin and death, and His promise to you now is, ' The gift of God is eternal life, through Jesus Christ our Lord.' ' They shall never perish ' " John 10. 28.

My Substitute

WHEN I was a boy, I saw a sight I never can forget—a man tied to a cart, and dragged before the people's eyes through the streets of my native town, his back torn and bleeding from the lash. It was a shameful punishment. For *many* offences? No; for ONE offence. Did any of the townsmen offer to divide the lashes with him? No; he who committed the offence bore the penalty alone.

When I was a student at the University, I saw another sight I can never forget—a man brought out to die. His arms were pinioned, his face was pale as death—thousands of eyes were upon him as he came up from the jail in sight. Did any man ask to die in his place? Did any friend come and loose the rope, and say, "Put it round my neck, and I will die in his stead?" No; he underwent the sentence of the law. For *many* offences? No; for **one** offence.

I saw another sight—(it matters not when)—myself a sinner, standing on the brink of ruin, deserving naught but hell. For *one* sin? No; for **many.** Many sins committed against the unchanging laws of God. But again I looked, and saw JESUS, **my Substitute, scourged in my stead,** and dying on the cross for me. I looked, and cried. I claimed Him as my Saviour, and was forgiven. I realized that He had taken my place—and thanked God for giving Him to die in my stead.

How simple it all becomes when God opens our eyes! The law demands justice; the Gospel delights in mercy, through satisfied justice. Moses blesses the law-doer; Jesus pardons the law-breaker, the guilty, and saves the lost.

"It's Got No Sting!"

A CROWD had gathered on the sea-shore, and, as is often usual, attracted others. On nearing it, we made our way through the outer edge, and were able to look over the heads of a number of boys who were intently gazing on a dangerous serpent which the showman had in his hands, and which curled round his arms and neck. A venomous snake, whose bite was of the deadliest ; but the man seemed to have charmed it, for though it shot out its forked tongue and touched him, it was quite harmless, and none of the evil effects we read of ensued. Most of the observers were amazed and puzzled, some not a little frightened, and various were the remarks made ; but at last one clever onlooker explained the cause of its doing no harm, and cried out, "Oh! it's got no sting." That was the solution. The sting, or venom bag, had been extracted, and the reptile rendered harmless.

Why are we afraid to die? Is it not on account of sin? We know assuredly that death is dreadful, and why? Because it has a sting. God says:—"The sting of death is sin." If only we could extract the sting, death would no longer be terrible. Who can extract the deadly poison? We cannot, but the Lord Jesus Christ has removed it already for all who are His. In Him "we have redemption through His blood, even the forgiveness of sins." "His own self bare our sins in His own body on the tree." And so death is swallowed up in victory. "O death, where is thy sting? O grave, where is thy victory? The sting of death is sin; and the strength of sin is the law. But thanks be to God, who giveth us the victory, through our Lord Jesus Christ."

NOW or NEVER

THERE are districts in the North where the inhabitants live, to a great degree, upon the eggs of sea-birds, which build their nests amongst the high precipitous rocks on the sea-coast and adjoining islands. One of these hunters was on one occasion at his usual calling, when he discovered a large nest, some hundred feet below him, upon a ledge of rock. The over-hanging rock from which he could see the nest made it very difficult to get at the spot, as, when letting himself down with a long rope, he would find it a difficult thing to get on to the rock, which was further inwards, underneath, than the peak upon which he stood.

However, these professional hunters are so accustomed to difficulties of the sort, he determined to try to reach the ledge. Accordingly, driving his large iron stake into the ground, and fixing his rope round it, he proceeded to let himself down over the cliff. Safely descending to the level of the nest, he was suspended in mid air by his rope. To reach the ledge, it was necessary to commence swinging to and fro. This is only done by action of the body ; but by degrees a heavy enough swing to and fro was obtained to touch, with his feet, the ledge of rock. The next swing back he determined to try and land safely upon the ledge. As he approached, it was necessary to give a spring, and balance himself, so as to enable him to stand upright upon the ledge. This was just the difficulty ; still, with skilled hands and steady brain, he safely accomplished it.

Partly congratulating himself, and not fully realizing his position, without thinking, just at that moment, by mistake he let go the rope. The coil and seat attached to it swung back with almost as great velocity as when he was in it.

In an instant he saw his position, and as quickly realized that little short of death stared him in the face. No one was above or near to let down another rope, or to accomplish the same feat, to reach the ledge, as he had just done himself. He saw the rope receding, and then again approaching him with a return swing. In cases of great danger, thought is often as **quick as lightning** in realizing necessity of action. He saw that if he did not give **a spring off** the ledge on to the rope on its next return swing, there might be **no hope** of catching it on the second return, as each time it would not come so near to him. With **one bound** just as the rope approached him, he sprang from the ledge, and, **saved** as it were from the very jaws of death, his presence of mind, and muscle enabled him to hang on to it, and once again get safely into the seat. He was rescued! Truly, it was **now** or **never**! He might have missed it, and been dashed to pieces upon the rocks some hundreds of feet again below him; but to save life we risk ALL.—My Soul, what is **thy** position?—Is it not—**Now or Never?**—To-morrow, perhaps, too late.

"He wasn't on for dying"

A NUMBER of young medical students were gathered in the dissecting-room of one of our large colleges, laughing and busily talking over the events of the day, for they happened to be many. Their work was done, for the time at least; and the ghastly remains before them threw no cloud over the merriment that was going on. No shadow, no reflection that perhaps soon, they too might be corpses, as still and helpless as the one over which they had just been occupied.

Foremost of the party was a young man whom we will call Edward Allen. Perhaps the noisiest of the party, the jests that fell from his lips were interspersed with names and expressions which he had no right to use so lightly, but which passed little heeded by his comrades, being too much accustomed to them. Indifferent to the solemn words he was uttering, he leant back against the wall, with the needle, which he had been using on the corpse before him, stuck carelessly into the facing of his coat. The conversation grew louder, and a hasty discussion was struck up on a trifling subject. As he was speaking, Allen lifted his hand with a careless gesture, and in doing so, caught it in the needle that was fastened in his coat, and gave his hand a deep tear. All were silent in a moment, then one of his companions remarked soberly: "I say, Allen, that's dangerous." "I know it is," he answered uneasily. "What shall I do?"

"Come to ——," they suggested, naming one of the chief doctors; and without delay they hurried off. It was an anxious moment as they stood waiting for his verdict; but it was unhesitatingly given. In a few words Edward Allen was told that he might possibly not be alive in twenty-four hours.

A man is brave when he is strong and well, even courageous when dashing into a battle-field, hoping by some "good luck" not to be touched; but when he is not ready to meet death, and the great doorway of Eternity quietly opens to receive him, his heart may fail. And thus despair seized Allen as his fate stared him in the face. We cannot relate the horrors of those last few hours, for he was dead in less than twenty-four. We can only repeat the words of one of his fellow-students. "It was dreadful to see him when he was told he might soon be gone, for he wasn't on for dying."

Perhaps **you** say—"not likely to happen to me"—Is it so? May be that death will meet you suddenly. Anyhow, are you prepared—that is the question.

I am Praying to God for Pardon

'I AM praying to God and trying to do my duty," said an old soldier. "Well, friend, what are you praying to God for?" was the reply. "Sir, I am praying to God for the pardon of my sins." "But do you expect to get pardon of your sins by praying?" "Yes, surely, for has He not told us to pray?" "True, He has told us to pray, but not for pardon of sin; that we get in another way." "How is that?" "By simply accepting the pardon He has given. When your wife offers you your tea, do you keep on asking for it or take it?" "Take it, certainly. Without asking."

"Well, then, just so take Christ's work of salvation,

already done for you, as the pardon for your sin. God says, 'Whosoever will, let him take the water of life freely.' It is not a question of asking or doing, but of taking—Christ; receiving Christ is the act of faith—that saves your soul."

How He Surrendered

CHARLES SIMEON, when young, read in a book that the Jews knew what they did, when they transferred their sin to the head of their offering. The thought rushed into his mind—What! may I transfer all my guilt to another? Has God provided an Offering for me, that I may lay my sins on His head? Then, God willing, I will not bear them on my own soul one moment longer; for I see that God laid my sins on Jesus.

BORN TWICE

By D. L. MOODY.

ONE of the finest specimens of a sincere worshipper was **startled** by Christ. He was confounded to think he must be **born again**. A great many people have this subject of regeneration a good deal mixed up. I have asked people if they were Christians, born again.

"Yes, I think so," they say.

"What makes you think so ?"

"Oh, I go regularly to church."

But that is no reason, for Satan goes to church. You may go to church, and yet be wicked and corrupt as any man.

Another class says, "I have been baptized." But baptism is not regeneration.

And then a great many say, "My father and mother were Christians; I was born a Christian." But God says otherwise.

The question is, "Have I been born of the Spirit ?" Christ told Nicodemus, "Except a man be born again, he cannot see the kingdom of God."

This question is so vast in importance that we should not be deceived. Take the Word of God, and look carefully—not into your own heart or experience, but into the Word, and see if you are born of God.

Nicodemus was not only a good man, but a teacher—what we call a preacher, a Doctor of Divinity—one of the best men in Jerusalem. Yet he came to Christ, and was startled when he was told that he must be born again—that all his righteousness and morality was, in the sight of God, like filthy rags. Nicodemus, like all others, had to commence at the bottom of the ladder.

"Must we not Work out our Salvation?"

"Does it not say in the Bible that we are to work out our salvation ? How then can you reconcile **that**, with the statement that we have only got to believe in order to be saved ?

Wait a moment. When you ask, "Does it not say we are to work out our salvation ?" whom do you mean ? Do you mean the saved or the unsaved ? Look at the Epistle (Phil. 1. 1), and see to whom it is addressed. " To the **saints** in Christ Jesus at Philippi." They were ALREADY saved. They did not **HOPE** to be saved, they knew they were saved. To **them** St. Paul said, " My beloved, . . . work out your own salvation " (Phil. 2. 12). " Your own " implies possession. They were to " work out " what God had already wrought IN.

VERY CLOUDY How many people have a cloudy idea of what salvation means. Let us quote four, when asked, " What must a person do to be saved ? "

From one, the answer will come, " Be honest and moral—pay your way."

From another, " Don't do anything wrong, and you will get to heaven ; treat every one the best you can."

Another will say, " Do as near right as you can, and pray to God."

And a fourth : " Don't swear, or lie, and don't do anything that you would be ashamed of."

To such replies we would inquire—What about the need of Atonement for sin ? God says all have sinned.

Loaded with Fetters

IT is told of a famous smith of Mediæval times, that having been taken prisoner and immured in a dungeon, he conceived the idea of escaping, and began to examine the chain that bound him, with a view to discover some flaw that might make it easier to be broken. His hope was vain, for he found, from marks upon it, that it was one of his own workmanship, and it had always been his boast that none could ever break a chain that he had forged. And now it was his *own* chain that bound him!

It is thus with the sinner. His own hands have forged the chain that binds him—a chain which no human hand can break. There is only one way of deliverance. Jesus can break the fetters—**Jesus alone**! Seek His help in your need. "If the Son make you free, ye shall be free indeed."

He breaks the power of cancelled sin,
He sets the prisoner free;
His blood can make the foulest clean,
His blood avails for me.

"John Three Sixteen"

or "The Watchword"

THERE was once a boy, a wandering City Arab, homeless, houseless, friendless. From childhood to boyhood he had been sinking into lower depths of misery, and it was ending in his becoming the associate of thieves. Weariness and terror often made him long for something else; but he was alone, hungry, and forlorn, and so he was becoming the slave of wicked men.

One dark cold night in November, he was awaiting his accomplices; the hour had not yet struck when the evil deed should take place—they had planned to commit a burglary in a house where the boy kept watch. The moon gleamed forth at intervals from the heavy clouds, and the robbers must wait until all was dark before they could attain their wicked purpose.

Brighter and brighter the moon shone forth, so bright that it cast a dark shadow on the boy's path as he hid himself behind the portico of the house.

Some one was there! Was it one of the thieves, to see if he were there? Was it the police, aware of their evil intentions?

No! A voice, not unkind, but with command in its tone, inquired, "Boy! what are you doing here so late? Go home, and go to bed; lads like you have no business in the streets at such an hour as this! Go home!" he repeated, as the boy did not move.

"I have no home to go to—no bed," replied the young Arab, and his voice trembled.

"Poor fellow," said the stranger compassionately; "would you go to a home and a bed if I procured you one?"

"That I would, gladly," replied the boy, as the cold north-east wind swept over his shivering frame, and carried the clouds away, so that the full light fell on the face of a gentleman, whose kindly smile shone brighter and warmer than moonlight on the heart of the wanderer. He gave the name of the street and the number, and the lad was hurrying off, when the gentleman recalled him.

"But how are you going to get in, my boy? You must have a pass-ticket, as well as an invitation, before you can be admitted. Take this; this is for you. Can you read?"

"No," replied the lad sadly. "I never learned."

"Well, remember on this ticket is 'John Three Sixteen.' Repeat it after me: 'John—Three—Sixteen.'"

He eagerly repeated it.

"Now do not forget, this is to give you a home and a bed, and is to do you good."

Off ran the lad with his precious ticket,

repeating his lesson without a moment's cessation, until he arrived breathlessly at the street door of the house indicated to him. He rang the bell fearlessly, for had not that kind friend told him, that John Three Sixteen would procure him a home and a bed, and do him good ? The night porter opened the door, and in a gruff voice inquired, " Who's there ? "

" It's me, please," gasped the boy. " Please, sir, I'M JOHN THREE SIXTEEN."

" All right ! " responded the porter ; " that's the pass for to-night. Come in."

The poor fellow soon found himself in a comfortable bed, his heart running over with gratitude for the shelter, not only from the cold night wind, but from his evil companions, and again and again he repeated, " I'll always be John Three Sixteen—it be so lucky."

He slept soundly until the morning, when he reluctantly left the place which had so wonderfully afforded him rest, food, and shelter solely on the strength of his new name.

He was again on the streets. Who knows how soon his evil associates would have enticed him to be again a partaker of their evil deeds, had not the Hand " mighty to save," snatched him from the mouth of the pit. In crossing a crowded thoroughfare he was run over by a cart, and carried to the nearest hospital. Before taking him into the ward he was asked :

" Are you a Protestant or a Romanist ? "

He did not understand anything about that : he only knew he was " John Three Sixteen."

" Well," said the warder, " he's very badly hurt ; carry him in—John Three Sixteen—or whatever his name is. Poor lad ! poor lad ! "

Men carried him into the accident ward, and laid him down tenderly, and watched him till the surgeon came, and often he whispered to himself as he laid there, " How lucky I am since I had my new name ; I'll always stick to it, that I am John Three Sixteen."

But soon everything was forgotten in his pain ; fever set in, and delirium followed ; but all the night long at intervals he repeated : " John Three Sixteen ; John Three Sixteen ! It was to do me good, and so it has."

Many a one in that ward, awakened by that ceaseless cry, stretched forth a feeble hand to turn the leaves of the Testament by their side, to learn what the continued repetition of the text meant. The Holy Spirit blessed it that night to several souls, for it was God's own Word, and He has promised that His Word shall not return unto Him void.

Oh ! how good it is that God's Word cannot lie ; that His promise can never change, and His Word endureth for ever. Try it. Prove Him. Believe Him.

Time went on. Our little lad awoke to new life. He gazed about him as he seemed to awake from a long sleep. Many eyes were fixed on him. At last a patient came from one of the beds nearest to him, and said, "John Three Sixteen! How are you?"

"How did you know my name?" inquired the boy eagerly.

"Know it, my lad! Why you have never ceased telling us of it; and I for one say, Blessed John Three Sixteen."

The boy marvelled how anyone could call him blessed, the poor Arab of the City, for whom no one had ever cared, before he had this new name. And then, for the first time in his life, he heard those life-giving words that had brought salvation to many, and were now ordained to bring life to him. "For God so loved the world, that He gave His only begotten Son, that whosoever believeth on Him should not perish, but have everlasting life."

Yes! he—poor orphan boy, who had early learned the bitter wages of sin, he, the companion of thieves, was saved, not condemned. "For God sent not His Son into the world to condemn the world; but that the world through Him might be saved" (verse 17).

Settled For Ever

"THANK God!—that is a relief," said a man, as his friend finished paying a bill for him. "It has lain on my mind for many a year, and cost me many a sleepless night. Yes, I do indeed feel it a relief; I shall sleep sound to-night."

It is indeed a relief to feel one's debts are paid, that no one has a claim against us, no fear of unwelcome visitors coming at awkward times, to make demands which it is impossible to meet. A friend who will pay our debts is a friend indeed, whom we cannot too highly value.

How much more precious is that friend, Jesus, the Saviour—who is waiting to pay our debt of sin, and settle it once and for ever. Those who have gone to Him with their burden of guilt, have found it removed, and been able to say, The Lord Jesus is able and willing to pay your debt, as He has paid the debts of thousands. The question is not one of amount, nor of how the debt was contracted, but only to let Him pay it.

STRUGGLING FOR LIFE

LAW presents a man struggling for life by obedience, but never obtaining it; GRACE presents a man receiving life as a free gift, through faith in the finished work of the Lord Jesus Christ.

Man's Way of Salvation

"There is a way which seemeth right unto a man, but the end thereof are the ways of death"—Prov. 14. 12.

"Going about to establish their own righteousness."—Romans 10. 3.

Morality: "I thank thee I am not as other men are."—Luke 18. 11.

Almsgiving: "I give tithes of all that I possess."—Luke 18. 12.

"We have made a covenant with death, and with hell are we at agreement."
—Isa. 28. 15.

Do not mistake, much that a man does, is right and proper; but if it is to be acceptable to God, it must be the outcome of life, after he has trusted in the finished work of Christ. What we do, must be the result of our forgiveness, not the means by which we try to obtain it.

God's Way of Salvation

Not of works, lest any man should boast.—Eph. 9. 2.

Christ died for the ungodly.—Rom. 5. 6.

The Just for the unjust. By Him all that believe are justified from all things.—Acts 13. 39.

Not redeemed with . . . silver and gold . . . but with the precious blood of Christ.—1 Pet. 1. 18.

His own self bare our sins in His own body on the tree.—1 Pet. 2. 24.

My sins deserve eternal death, but Jesus died for me.

MAN'S GREATEST NEED

A man may lack liberty, and yet be happy; a man may lack food, and yet be content; a man may lack clothing, and yet be comfortable; but he that lacks Salvation, lacks everything that can do him good, in this life and the next. Nothing worse can be imagined, than to be without hope and without God even in this world.

When the Bee Stung Mother

A YOUNG man was once asked by his minister, how long he had known his Saviour, and if he knew his sins were forgiven.

" Oh, yes," he replied ; " I know that they are all forgiven ; I am sure of that."

" When did you first come to know and understand that ? " asked the minister.

" When the bee stung mother," he replied.

" When the bee stung mother ? Tell me what you mean."

" Sir," said he, " I had a mother who in my boy days had often told me what Jesus had done for me ! but I never really understood and realized how He had taken my place, and died in my stead, **until** one summer's afternoon, when playing at the door of our cottage. Mother was ironing near the kitchen door, with her sleeves turned up. Suddenly, a large and excited bee came buzzing round and round my head. It no doubt had been hurt, and seemed determined to sting. I was frightened, and tried once or twice to flap it away with my handkerchief ; but round it came, closer each time. At last, in despair, I ran inside to get rid of my enemy, and made for my mother, who had been watching me ; and with a cry I hid myself under her long apron. Amused at my fear, but with motherly care, and a smile she put her arms outside the apron as it were to assure me that I was safe.

" This was hardly done, before the bee settled upon her bare arm and stung her so deeply that the poor thing was hardly able to draw out its sting. My mother, who felt the sting sharply, was taken aback; but looking at the bee she said to me, 'There, you may come out now; **the bee has stung mother instead of you;** come out and look at it crawling on mother's arm. It cannot hurt you now, it has only one sting!"

" Half afraid, and sorry for my mother, I looked at the sting whilst my mother well applied the lesson, explaining to me how it was a picture of what for long she had told me, about Jesus having taken my place, and had been punished in my stead. I had learned and often repeated that verse, 'By His stripes we are healed,' but **I never understood till then,** with the bee and sting before us, that it was indeed just what Jesus had permitted to be done to Himself—punished instead of us. That moment of realization! I shall never forget it. It was all so clear now. I saw and understood for the first time what mother had for long taught me, how that God would not punish me, because He had already punished Jesus in my stead. Yes, sir, it was when the bee stung mother. I have rejoiced from that moment in believing and being assured that Jesus died for me on Calvary."

“I’m Going by the Book”

TWO men, the one a foreman, the other one of the carpenters under him, were standing on the deck of a steamship then on the stocks, in one of the ship-building yards on the Clyde.

“Well, S——,” said the foreman, “I have been anxious to have a conversation with you. I’m told you are one of those people who say they know for certain that they are saved. Is that true?”

“Yes,” said S——, “quite true; thank God, I know I’m saved; in fact, there is nothing I’m more sure of, than that I’m saved.”

“Well, now,” said the foreman, “that is something I cannot see through, how any man can say that he is saved as long as he is in this world. I think it is rather presumptuous for any one to say so.

“I used to attend Mr. ——’s place of worship, a good many years ago, and several of the leading men in it pressed on me to become a member, but I could not, for I knew I was not a Christian, and told them so. In fact, I was disgusted with them. I knew so many who went to that place, and pretended to remember the death of Christ, who were just as bad as I was. I left them, and have never gone to any place since, for I concluded the whole thing was a sham, and that there was no reality in Christianity at all."

"Well," said S——, "I'm not at all surprised at you, but there *is a reality in being saved,* in being a child of God, and in knowing it. What is the breadth of this waterway ?" The foreman, astonished at the apparently sudden change in the conversation, said, "Why, 14 inches all round, to be sure; what makes you ask that, when you know ?"

"But are you quite sure that it is to be 14 inches ?" said S——.

"Certainly."

"But what makes you so sure ?" asked S——.

"*Why, I'm going by the book,*" and, as he said so, he pulled a book out of his pocket, in which were marked the sizes and position of the various things on the deck. "I'm sure it is 14 inches, for it is here in the book, and I got the book from headquarters."

"Oh! I see," said S——; "now look here; that is exactly how I know I'm saved. *I'm just going by the Book.* It came from headquarters—it is God's Word. I found in here that I was a lost, condemned sinner, worthy of nothing but the Lake of Fire; but I also found that 'God so loved the world, that He gave His only begotten Son, that whosoever believeth in Him should not perish, but have everlasting life' (John 3. 16). I took God at His Word, and I'm saved; and you, too, may be saved if you will, simply as you are, a lost, condemned sinner. Believe in Jesus; that is, trust Him as your Saviour, and you are saved; and then you can say without presumption, I *know* I'm saved, for *I'm going by the Book.*"

Reader, can you say, on the authority of God's Word, "I know I'm saved"? Profession without the new birth will never take you to heaven. Before it is too late, hear the voice of Jesus calling, "Come unto Me, all ye that labour and are heavy laden, and I will give you rest" (Matt. 11. 28). "He that heareth My word, and believeth on Him that sent Me, hath everlasting life" (John 5. 24).

The Sinner's Surety

FROM whence this fear and
    unbelief
If God, my God, hath put to
    grief
  His spotless Son for me?
Can He, the righteous Judge of
    men,
Condemn me for that debt of
    sin,
  Which, Lord, was charged on
    Thee?
If Thou hast my discharge pro-
    cured
And freely in my place endured
  The whole of wrath Divine,
Payment God will not twice
    demand
First at my bleeding Surety's
    hand,
  And then again at mine.

David pleaded: "O remember not against us former iniquities." Ps. 79. 8.

God answers: "I, even I, am He that blotteth out thy transgressions for Mine own sake, and will not remember thy sins." Is. 43. 35.

TAKING *v.* ASKING

I ASKED a farmer one day, whether he had salvation in Christ. " No, indeed, sir, I have not, but my wife and I are both very anxious for it. There's not a day of our lives but we read a chapter in the Bible at night, and we ask God to give it to us."

" You ask God to give it to you ? "

" Yes, sir, indeed we do."

"You are quite wrong," I added. " Your business is to take it. God is asking you to be reconciled. What business have you asking God for salvation, or to be reconciled to you, when He says here, He ' was in Christ, reconciling the world unto Himself ' ? I want you to take Him at His word, and rest on the finished work of Christ for sin."

" And do you mean to say, sir,

that I have not even to ask for it?"

"No, for the work is finished, and God wants you to believe Jesus' blood is an atonement for your sin."

"Well, sir, I never thought of that before, that it was so free I hadn't even to ask for it. I do believe in Jesus, that His death is sufficient for all my sins."

"And Jesus tells you that 'he that believeth on Me hath everlasting life.'"

"I see it all now, sir; I never saw it before."

Some months after, I met him, a happy believer, by taking the gift of God—eternal life—instead of going on asking for it. He said his wife had accepted it too, and now they didn't ask God for salvation, but they just **thanked** Him for it.

"Admit the Bearer —a Sinner"

"SO, John, you've got fairly into the kingdom. You have been long seeking; how did you get in at last?"

"Oh, it was the simplest thing in the world; it was just by presenting the right ticket. I held it out, the door was opened, and I was in. And the strange thing is, I found that the ticket of admission had been in my possession from childhood, and I had carried it in my pocket for the last twelve months, and never had the sense to use it."

"That is strange, for you were so anxious to get in. What kind of a ticket was it, and what was written on it?"

"Why, it was as plain a ticket as you ever bought for a public meeting; it had nothing on it but the words,—

> "ADMIT THE BEARER
>
> A SINNER"
>
> Luke 18. 13, 14.

"Was that all?" "Yes. And what

kept me so long from getting in was, that I always *added* something to the words on the ticket, when I presented it. Whenever the Lord saw anything of my adding, it was refused. The first time I went, I wrote at the bottom, 'But not so great a sinner as many of my neighbours.' That would not do, so I rubbed it out and put down, 'But is doing the best he can to improve.' That would not do, either, so I became anxious, and prayed and wept awhile, and then, under the words, 'Admit the bearer, a sinner,' I wrote, 'Who is praying and weeping for his sins.' Even that wouldn't do. After that I began to despair, and wrote down, 'Too great a sinner to be saved.' That only made matters worse, and I had almost given up, when I looked at Christ and heard Him say, 'Him that cometh to Me I will in no wise cast out' (John 6. 37.) and those precious words, 'Whosoever will, let him take of the water of life freely' (Rev. 22. 17). I remembered that Jesus had said, 'I came to call sinners to repentance,' so I pulled out the old ticket, and, without adding a word, presented it, was accepted, and I entered."

GO THOU AND DO LIKEWISE

Story of an Artist's Studio

YEARS ago, a painter stood in his studio, his right thumb to the belt of his blouse, and his left hand holding the pipe he had withdrawn from his lips, in honour of his visitor, Father Hugo, the Vicar of the rich Church of St. Jerome. The artist had not yet reached middle age. He was famous in Düsseldorf, and some said that his name would some day be known world-wide. When that day came, Stenburg ruefully thought that he would be past the enjoyment of riches which tarried so long. Still, he managed to enjoy life in the present. He loved his art. Now and again he became so absorbed in his work, that he forgot all else than the picture upon his easel.

Still, though good work he had done, he had as yet never satisfied himself, nor reached his own ideal. His was good work, but he desired something more. Thus Stenburg was not a satisfied man. Otherwise, to the world, he appeared a jolly, prosperous man, who displayed, on occasion, a shrewd business capacity, and one who knew his own interests well. He was speaking now.

" No, Reverend Father ; the sum you offer would but ill repay me for the labour of so large an altar-piece as you honour me by naming. It must have many figures, all carefully studied. The crucifixion is not an easy subject, and it has been so often taken, that it would be difficult to compose a picture different—as I should wish it to be—from others."

"I will not limit you to the price. You are an honest man, Sir Painter, and the Church of St. Jerome will not pay for the altar-piece. It is to be the gift of a penitent."

"So! That makes a difference. Return, Reverend Father, a month from to-day, and studies for the work shall be ready."

They parted, both well pleased, and during the following weeks Stenburg studied the composition of the altar-piece, and penetrated into the Jewish Strasse for models for his figures.

Father Jerome was satisfied. He desired the central point of the picture to be the Cross of the Redeemer, and left the grouping of the accessories to the artist. From time to time the Vicar dropped in to inspect the progress of the work.

With the bursting of the young green leaves, and the upspringing of the first flowers, a hunger had seized upon the artist's soul to leave Düsseldorf, and with his sketch-book wander over the surrounding country. On the borders of the forest he came one day upon a gipsy girl plaiting straw baskets. Her face was beautiful; her coal-black hair fell in waving ripples to her waist; and her poor, tattered, red dress, faded and sunburnt to many hues, added to her picturesque appearance. But her eyes were the feature that caught the artist's regard,—restless, limpid, black eyes, whose expression changed every moment : pain, joy, fun, and roguery were reflected in their depths as swiftly as the cloud shadows chase each other across a lake.

" What a capital picture she would make ! " thought Stenburg ; " but then, who would buy a gipsy girl ? No one ! "

The gipsies were looked upon in Düsseldorf with hatred, and even to this day the fact of being a gipsy is, in the eyes of the law, a punishable offence.

The girl noticed the artist, and, flinging her straw down, sprang up, raising her hands above her head, and, snapping her fingers to keep time, danced lightly and gracefully before him, showing her white teeth, her glance sparkling with merriment.

" Stand ! " cried Stenburg, and he rapidly sketched her. Quickly as he drew, it was a weary position for the girl to maintain ; but she never flinched, though a sigh of relief, as her arms dropped and she stood at rest before him, attested to the artist the strain the attitude had been.

" She is not only beautiful, she is better—a capital model. I will paint her as a Spanish dancing-girl."

So a bargain was struck. Pepita was to come thrice a week to Stenburg's house to be painted. Duly at the appointed hour she arrived. She was full of wonder. Her great eyes roved round the studio, glancing on the pieces of armour, pottery, and carving. Presently she began examining the pictures,—and soon the great altar-piece, now nearing its completion, caught her attention. For days she gazed at it intently. At last in an awed voice she asked :—

"Who is that ?" pointing to the most prominent figure.

"The Christ," answered Stenburg carelessly.

"What is being done to Him ?"

"Being crucified," ejaculated the artist. "Turn a little to the right. There ! that will do."

Stenburg, with his brush in his fingers, was a man of few words.

"Who are those people about Him—those with the bad faces ?"

"Now, look here," said the artist, "I cannot talk to you. You have nothing to do but stand as I tell you."

The girl dare not speak again, but she continued to gaze and speculate. Every time she came to the studio the fascination of the picture grew upon her. Sometimes she ventured an inquiry, for her curiosity consumed her.

"Why did they crucify Him ? Was He bad, very bad ?" "No ; very good."

That was all she learnt at one interview, but she treasured each word,—and every sentence was so much more known of the mystery.

"Then, if He was good, why did they do

so ? Was it for a short time only ? Did they let Him go ? "

" It was because——." The artist paused with his head on one side, stepped forward, and arranged her sash.

" Because," repeated Pepita breathlessly.

The artist went back to his easel ; then looking at her, the eager, questioning face moved his pity.

" Listen. I will tell you once for all, and then ask no further questions " ; and he told her the story of the Cross—new to Pepita, though so old to the artist, that it had ceased to touch him. He could paint that dying agony, and not a nerve of his quivered ; but the thought of it wrung her heart. Her great black eyes swam in tears, which the fiery gipsy pride forbade to fail.

The altar-piece and the Spanish dancing-girl were finished simultaneously. Pepita's last visit to the studio had come. She looked upon the beautiful representation of herself without emotion, but turned and stood before the altar-piece, unable to leave it.

" Come," said the artist, " here is your money, and a gold piece over and above, for you have brought me good luck, the ' Dancing-girl ' is already sold : I shall want you some time perhaps again, but we must not over-stock the market with even your pretty face."

The girl turned slowly. " Thanks, Signor ! " but her eyes, full of emotion, were solemn. " You must love Him *very* much, Signor, when He has **done all that for you,** do you not ? "

The face into which she looked flushed crimson. The artist was ashamed. The girl, in her poor, faded dress, passed from his studio, but her plaintive words rang in his heart. He tried to forget them, but impossible. He hastened to send the picture to its destination ; still he could not forget,—" **all that for you**."

At last the pain was not to be borne. He would face it and conquer it. He went to confession ; Father Hugo questioned Stenburg. He believed all the doctrines of the Church. So the Vicar gave him absolution, and assured him that " all was well." The artist allowed a liberal discount on his altar-piece, and for a week or two felt at ease. But then up rose the old question, " You must love Him very much, do you not ? " and **would** be answered. He grew restless, and could not settle to his work. So wandering about he heard of things which had not come under his notice before. One day he saw a group of persons hastening to a house near the walls, a poor place, and then he noticed others coming in the opposite direction, and they, too, passed into its low doorway. He asked what was happening there, but the man he questioned could not satisfy him. This roused his curiosity.

A few days later he learned that a stranger, one of the " Reformed," lived there—one of those despised men who appealed on every occasion to the Word of God. It was hardly respectable, hardly safe, even to know them. Yet perhaps here he might find that which he sought. They might possess the secret of peace. So Stenburg went to observe, perhaps to inquire, certainly not to join them ; but a man cannot approach fire and remain cold. This Reformed preacher spoke and looked as one who was walking on earth with Christ ; yes, one to whom He was all. Stenburg found what he longed for—**a living faith.** His new friend lent him for a time a precious copy of the New Testament, but, hunted from Düsseldorf after a few weeks, he left, and had to take the Book with him ; but its essence was left in Stenburg's heart.

Ah ! no need to question now. He felt in his soul the fire of an ardent love. " Did all that for me ! How can I ever tell men of that love, that boundless love, which can brighten their lives, as it has mine ? It is for them too, but they do not see it, as I did not. How can I preach it ? I cannot speak. I am a man of few words. If I were to try I could never speak it out. It burns in my heart, but I cannot express it—*the love of Christ!* " So thinking, the artist idly drew with a piece of charcoal in his fingers a rough sketch of a thorn-crowned head. His eyes grew moist as he did so. Suddenly the thought flashed through his soul, " I can paint ! My brush must proclaim it. Ah ! in that altar-piece His face was all agony. But that was not the truth. Love unutterable, infinite compassion, willing sacrifice ! "

The artist fell on his knees, and prayed to paint worthily, and thus speak.

And then he wrought. The fire of genius blazed up—up to the highest fibre of his power ; nay, beyond it. The new picture of the crucifixion was a wonder—almost Divine.

He would not sell it. He gave it a free-will offering to his native city, Düsseldorf. It was hung in the public gallery, and there the citizens flocked to see it, and voices were hushed and hearts melted as they stood before it, and the burghers returned to their homes knowing the love of God, and repeating to themselves the words written so distinctly beneath—

> **"All this I did for thee;**
> **What hast thou done for Me?"**

Stenburg also used to go there, and, watching far back from the corner in the gallery the people who gathered about the picture, he prayed God to bless his painted sermon. One day he observed, when the rest of the visitors had left, a poor girl standing weeping bitterly before it. The artist approached her. "What grieves thee, child ?" he asked.

The girl turned : she was Pepita. "Oh ! Signor, **if He had but loved me so,**" she said, pointing to the face of yearning love, bending above them. "I am only a poor gipsy. For **you** is the love, but not for such as **I**" ; and her despairing tears fell unrestrained.

"Pepita, **it was also all for thee.**" And then the artist told her all. Until the late hour at which the gallery closed they sat and talked. The painter did not weary now of answering her questions, for the subject was one he loved. He told the girl the story of that wondrous life, magnificent death, and crowning glory of resurrection, and also explained to her the union which that redeeming love effected. She listened, received, and believed these words,—

"All this I did for thee."

* * * *

Years after, when both the painter and the gipsy girl had met in another land above, a gay young nobleman drove in his splendid equipage into Düsseldorf, and, while his horses were baited, wandered into that famous gallery. He was rich, young, intelligent,—the world bright, and its treasures within his grasp. He stood before Stenburg's picture, arrested.

"All this I did for thee;
What hast thou done for Me?"

He read and re-read the legend on the frame. He could not tear himself away,—it grew into his heart. The love of Christ laid its powerful grasp on his soul. Hours passed; the light faded; the curator had to touch the weeping nobleman and tell him it was time to close the gallery. Night had come,—nay! rather, for that young man, the dawn of eternal Life. He was Zinzendorf. He returned to the Inn and re-entered his carriage, but to turn his back on Paris, and seek again his home. From **that** moment he threw life, fortune, fame, at the feet of HIM who he realized had died for him.

Zinzendorf, the father of the wonderful Moravian Missions, answered that question by his devoted life and welcomed death.

Stenburg's picture no longer hangs in the gallery at Düsseldorf, for when some years ago the gallery was destroyed by fire, it perished; but it preached, and God used it to tell of His gift, of whom St. Paul said, "He loved me and gave Himself for me."

Can you say—"and for me"?

"I gave my life for thee;
My precious blood I shed,
That thou might'st ransomed be,
And quickened from the dead.
I gave My life for thee:
What hast thou given for Me?

"I spent long years for thee,
In weariness and woe,
That an eternity of joy
Thou mightest know.
I spent long years for thee:
Hast thou spent one for Me?"

'Thank You, Captain!'

A REVIEW of his army by the first Napoleon was no ordinary scene. He was a conqueror, and he looked with pride on the human instruments of his victories. His soldiers believed in him with unquestioning faith, and followed him with enthusiastic devotion.

But it happened on one such occasion of imperial display that, while occupied in giving an order, the emperor incautiously let the rein fall upon the neck of his horse, which, taking fright, darted off at a gallop, placing the rider in imminent danger of being thrown.

While all stood gazing in consternation, a private soldier, from his place in the ranks, sprang before the horse, seized the bridle, and respectfully placed the reins in the hand of the emperor.

"Thank you, *captain*," said the rescued emperor, as quick to reward as to apprehend a service.

"*Of what regiment, sire?*" asked the soldier, saluting him.

"Of my own guards," replied the emperor, charmed with such a manifestation of faith in his sincerity, and he then galloped away.

Instantly acting on the declaration, the soldier laid down his gun, intimated his new rank to his companions, and passed over to the group of staff officers.

" What does the fellow want ? " haughtily asked one.

" The fellow," said the soldier, " is a captain of the emperor's guards."

" A captain ! " cried another. " Who said so ? "

" *He* said so," replied the soldier, pointing to the emperor ; on which the officers immediately greeted him as one of themselves.

Would it not have been more discreet, more modest, to wait and see if the emperor took any further steps in the matter, for such a piece of good fortune seemed really too good to be true ? No ! the truest discretion was to *believe* that the emperor meant what he said, the truest modesty was to receive unquestioningly the grace bestowed, and obediently accept its conditions.

Enfolded, parable-wise, in this incident lies a great spiritual lesson.

A wonderful word has been spoken,

and wonderful results are to follow for all who *believe* it.

"God so loved the world, that He gave His only begotten Son, that *whosoever believeth* in Him should not perish, but have everlasting life."

It is a familiar sentence, to be heard in every place where the Gospel is proclaimed.

On the simple fact of belief or unbelief hangs the power and consequence of the whole declaration.

Shall a little earthly dignity be instantly accepted on the word of an earthly sovereign, a despot, a tyrant, because he is understood to mean what he says, and has power to fulfil it ? and shall the word of the King of kings, the Lord of the whole earth, who died to purchase the right so to bestow, be doubted, and rejected ? Is not such rejection presumptuous and absurd ?

But once appropriating individually the blessed "whosoever," once over the Rubicon of "believeth in Him," there is no limit to the sinner's welcome, the saint's inheritance. "All things are" then "yours, for ye are Christ's, and Christ is God's."

ONLY TWO WAYS

ONLY 2 WAYS:

The broad and the narrow:
One downward, the other upward;
One to destruction, the other to life;
One taken by many, the other by few.

Which is Yours?

ONLY 2 SORTS OF PEOPLE:

Saved sinners, and unsaved sinners;
The chaff, or the wheat;
The sheep, or the goats;
The living, or the dead.

Which are You?

ONLY 2 DEATHS:

That of the righteous, that of the wicked;
That of the saved, that of the lost.

Which will be Yours?

ONLY 2 FUTURES:

Come ye blessed; These to Life Eternal.	Depart, ye cursed; These to Everlasting Punishment.

What will be Yours?

You can settle NOW, which or what. Soon, it will be too late.

The Lady and the Fruit

A GENTLEMAN, returning from market in an omnibus, was carrying in his hand a small basket of choice fruit; shortly, a lady entered, and, seeing the fruit, freely expressed her admiration of its beauty and excellence, adding, how glad she would have been to have bought some like it, that she might have had the pleasure of presenting it to friends whom she was going to visit.

The gentleman at once very courteously offered it for her acceptance. Much, however, as she would have liked to have the fruit, she would not accept it as a gift from a stranger, though she would gladly take it, she said, if he would permit her to **pay for it.** That, however, he declined, though still expressing his willingness to give it to her.

During some further conversation, the lady continued to show a desire to have the fruit, if by purchase. At last, the gentleman brought the matter to a close thus :—"Well, ma'am," said he, "I must tell you that you must either have it **as a gift or not at all.**" She at length agreed to take it as he offered it, cheerfully acknowledging his kindness.

Just like man! He fancies he can do something for or towards his own salvation, and is unwilling to accept eternal life from God as a gift. If you will not receive salvation as the gift of God, you cannot have it at all, but must perish in your sins.

The Helpless Helped

The Lord takes up none but the **forsaken.**
Makes none healthy but the **sick,**
Gives sight to none but the **blind,**
Makes none alive but the **dead,**
Saves none but sinners.

The Watchword

IN one of the rock galleries of Gibraltar, two British soldiers had mounted guard, one at each end of a tunnel. One was a Christian, the other was seeking Christ. It was midnight; and as the soldiers were going their rounds, one meditating on the blood of Christ which had brought him peace, the other brooding over his doubts and fears, suddenly an officer challenged the Christian soldier, and demanded the password. "The precious blood of Christ," called out aloud the startled soldier, forgetting the watchword in the thoughts of his heart. Immediately he corrected himself, and gave the watchword; and the officer, amazed, passed on. But these words had run through the rock galleries, and, echoed by the solid walls, had struck upon the ear of the doubting and seeking soldier as a messenger from heaven. It seemed as if an angel had spoken with words direct from the throne. "The precious blood of Christ." "Yes," he said, "that is just what I need."

ARE ALL SINNERS?

ONCE in this country there was a game that used to be played with bow and arrows. A man had to shoot ten arrows through a hoop at a distance. If he missed one he was called a "sinner"; if he missed more than one, or all of them, still he was called by the same name, a sinner. God says, "Whosoever shall keep the whole law and yet offend in ONE point, he is guilty of ALL."

No man objects to be called a sinner, but call him a criminal, and he is greatly offended. Why? The one has sinned against God, the other has sinned against man.

One Thing Needful. Have You Got It?

MANY things are useful and desirable. Only one thing is absolutely indispensable. There is only one thing which, if a man possess, he is **well off,** whatever else he may lack; only one thing which, if a man lack, he is ruined, whatever else he may possess.

Is it property? No; for we have seen persons utterly destitute of it, and yet happy and contented.

Is it health? Many persons have had their happiest hours in severe sickness. Health is not indispensable.

Is it a good reputation? The consciousness of innocence will uphold a man against the wildest storm of obloquy. A good man, whom slanderers have made hateful to his fellow-men, is far happier than he, whom successful hypocrisy has led his fellow-men to load with honours. "A good name is better than rubies,"—but—even a good name is not the one thing **indispensable.**

An interest in Jesus Christ, an experimental knowledge of His great salvation, is the only INDISPENSABLE thing. You cannot do without this. You cannot meet God without it. You cannot stand at the judgment-seat without it. It is "the one thing needful"—the one indispensable thing.

HAVE YOU GOT IT ?

Safe, Then Happy

"OH, sir, I think I understand the Gospel now, and believe it, yet I am not as happy as I expected."

"Why, friend, you are away after your feeling. Remember, it is not written, He that believeth, and is happy, shall be saved, but 'Whosoever believeth shall be saved,' whether happy or not. The greater thing is to be safe rather than happy; but when we **know** that we **are** safe in Jesus, we are sure to be happy.

"Suppose, now, that you were in debt, and in fear about it, not being able to pay it, and suppose I should say, I am sorry to see you in this state, let us try to cheer you up, by singing some cheerful song. Would you not reply, 'That will not do; you might make me happy thus; still, they would put me in jail, unless the debt was paid' ? What is wanted is to know that the debt is paid ; when that is done, you are safe, and then are sure to be happy, because safe. Has not Jesus paid the debt ? answered for the crime ? met all claims against you ? Is not Jehovah satisfied with the work of Christ ? and what has satisfied **Him** ought to satisfy **you**."

WHICH?

IN the Cathedral at Worcester, there is an ancient slab, bearing as its inscription the solitary word: MISERRIMUS,—" Most Miserable."

Down in the Catacombs—those vast underground chambers of the dead, where the early Christians endeavoured to hide from their fierce persecutors—engraven on a stone embedded in the wall, stands this beautiful word, " FELICISSIMUS "—"*Most Happy.*"

If *you* **were to be laid in your grave this week, which of those Latin inscriptions would most truly represent your condition ?**

The Astonished Slave

A BRITISH merchant, who had taken his passage in a Turkish vessel on the Levant, had his attention drawn, during the voyage, to an interesting slave, a Mussulman. He got into conversation with him, and found him intelligent, quick, and of strong, lively affections. He drew from him some particulars of his history, and found that he had been free-born, but had been made captive in war. The merchant was touched with sympathy for this helpless captive. The more he knew of him, the deeper was the interest he felt in his welfare ; and he actually began to entertain the thought of effecting his release. Cautiously inquiring as to the sum requisite for this purpose, he found that it was considerably greater than the mercantile profits of his entire voyage. Still he could not abandon the thought. An offer was made and at last accepted ; but the slave having overheard part of the conversation and mistaking the design of the foreign merchant—supposing that he was purchasing him for his own use abroad—he sprang forward, his eyes gleaming with indignation, and cried out, "And do you call yourself a free-born Briton, an enemy to slavery, and yet purchase me? Have I not as much right to freedom as you have yourself ?"

He was proceeding in this strain of burning, indignant invective, when the merchant turned his eyes affectionately upon him and said, "***I have bought you, to set you free.***" Instantly the storm of passion was hushed : the slave burst into tears, and, falling at the feet of his deliverer, said : "**You have taken my heart captive! I am your willing slave for ever!**"

Reader,—When first you heard of One who wished to have you for His own, did you rebel,—oppose His purchase ? How little you realized it was out of pure love for you! Does not your heart break as you think of these words, "to set you free" the price was paid ; and can you but say to the One who gave His life for you—

***"I am your slave for ever"* (?)**

God says: "Ye are bought with a price" (1 Cor. 6. 20)—"purchased with His own blood" (Acts 20. 28)—"redeemed with the precious blood of Christ" (1 Pet. 1. 19).

IN A RING OF FIRE

AN ungodly European was once trying to convince a Christian convert in India that his religion was of no use, and that he never would be any the better for it. "What, after all," said the scoffer, "has your Jesus done for you?"

"He has saved me!" said the native, with great animation.

"And what is that?" said the European, with an incredulous smile.

"Step with me to the door," was the reply, "and I will show you." So saying, he took him outside, picked up a quantity of dry leaves (of which there were plenty close at hand), and made a large circle of them. He then sought for a worm; and, having found one, he placed it in the centre of the ring. Forthwith he applied a lighted match to the material that surrounded it, the scoffer looking on with no little astonishment. As the heat of the fire approached the poor worm, it began to writhe and to show symptoms of distress, but could not get out of the smouldering ring. The man darted his hand through the smoke, plucked the worm out of its dangerous position, and placed it on the green grass, out of reach of all danger.

"There," said he, "**that** is what the **blessed Jesus has done for me.** I was exposed to the flames of hell—there was no possibility of escape; I was condemned and ready to perish, and He rescued me by dying for my sins, snatching me as a brand from the burning; and He has given me (a poor dying worm) a place near His heart." We need not say the officer was silenced.

Can you thus speak of yourself as ***saved*** by the death of Jesus? Are you able to say, like the poor native, "***He has saved me***"? If not, we entreat you, as a sinner, to come now to Jesus, and He will give ***you*** rest. Take shelter in His blood, and ***you*** will be delivered from the wrath to come.

"When we were yet without strength, in due time Christ died for the ungodly" (Rom. 5. 6). "Thou hast in love to my soul delivered it from the pit of corruption" (Isa. 38. 17). "Ye were as a firebrand plucked from the burning" Amos. 4. 11).

The Seven Wonders

THE seven wonders of the world. What are they ? There are a great many strange and wonderful things in this world so the seven chief ones must be great and famous.

" What are they ? " we ask again with no small interest. " How is it that everybody does not know all about them ? "

After research in ancient books, we hear the list of long names which we can scarcely understand. The Pyramids of Egypt, the Colossus of Rhodes, and five other names, some of heathen temples, or statues of false gods. And what are they to us ?

Some of them are crumbling away to ruin ; and those that remain will be of small account in the day when God says, " heaven and earth shall pass away." Has it ever brought comfort to the troubled heart or peace to the dying bed ? Have tears been dried, or has rest of heart been given by the recollections of seven such wonders ? Why, half the people in the world have never heard of their existence ; and many have forgotten their names ! But we have **ANOTHER WONDER** to tell you about, one that infinitely surpasses any wonder of earth ; one, too, which concerns **you**—yes, you who are reading these words—a wonder that can bring joy to you now, and that can supply all your future need.

Listen! it is this: that—"God so loved the world, that He gave His only begotten Son, that whosoever believeth in Him should not perish, but have everlasting life" (John 3. 16).

Who loved the world?—God? Yes: God, who had so much that was pure and fair that He might have loved! All the hosts of heaven. They were sinless. Why should He love the world, this black, lost, ungrateful world? One of you might take up some vile and degraded stranger from the streets, and lavish **kindness** upon him, but you would not **love** him, especially if he repaid your kindness with base ingratitude, hating you, often seeking to drag your name in the dust—in an oath. Nay, more—would you, if this wretch incurred the penalty of the law and forfeited his life for some crime—would you give your only child **to take his place**?

The picture is not half drawn; it is only a feeble outline of the real fact,—the wonder of the world—that we have to tell you about. **You**, yes you, are the lost wanderer, the ungrateful wretch; and it is the God of heaven who gave His only Son to die for **you**. When you had so fairly earned the wages of sin, which is death, he—the Lord Jesus—**gave His life as your substitute, and shed His blood in your stead.** The greatest Wonder of the World.

For The Ungodly

IT does not say, for Thomas Smith or James Brown, but that " Christ died for the ***ungodly***." Say, would you not rather have it thus ? But do not suppose that because Christ died for the ungodly, therefore all the ungodly will be saved. Such reasoning would be very shallow. Were the King to charter a fleet of ships to take all the poor to New Zealand free, and then send forth a proclamation that on a certain day the ships will sail, we know that all the poor would not go, though it was open for them to do so. Many might ; but others would prefer to remain in poverty. The vessels were there to take them, but they would not go. In the same way " Christ died for the ungodly," but His death ONLY shields from judgment, as many as believe, accept Christ as their substitute.

LIFE AND HAPPINESS

WE can get life and happiness only in Christ. Apart from Him all is death and misery..

CHRIST AS A SAVIOUR
THE SAVIOUR
MY SAVIOUR

Three words, short, clear, different in meaning.

"A" is the indefinite article, very indefinite indeed; a Saviour, but not mine,—not for me—for some one else;—whose,—I know not.

"THE" is the definite article,—the Saviour, that is, the only one—not any other;—no other helper or refuge;—the world knows there is only one.

"MY" is a personal pronoun,—my Saviour—appropriated by me,—has saved me.—So we see,—

CHRIST as A Saviour shows the need.

CHRIST as THE Saviour, showing there is but one.

CHRIST as MY Saviour shows that He is mine.

The Broken Safe and the Discovered Will

A YOUNG man in America, the son of a wealthy Christian man, had become wayward and extravagant in his habits ; and finally, quarrelling with his father because he had refused him all the money he demanded, had left home in anger, and given himself up to a reckless life. For a long time he continued an abandoned wanderer. Becoming at one time very straitened, and being brought to the verge of desperation, he determined to break into his father's house in the absence of the family, thinking, since he knew well where the valuables were kept, that he could find means to relieve his necessity. " My father owes me a living," he said to himself, " and I will have it ! "

He succeeded in effecting an entrance into the house and safe, and, amid the stillness of the house, began his search. Coming upon some valuable papers, he found, amongst the rest,

HIS FATHER'S WILL.

With curious eye he began reading that will. To his utter astonishment he found his name among the heirs, and a large bequest set against it. At first he could hardly credit his eyes. The father with whom he had quarrelled, against whom he had cherished such bitterness—could it be possible that he had retained his name in his Will, and was yet intending to give him his portion with the rest ? " Can it be," he said to himself, " that

my father loves me, in spite of all my hatred and bitterness toward him ?

"Can it be that, in spite of the dishonour I have brought upon him, he is still ready to treat me as a son ?" And such was the effect of these thoughts, that they were the means of bringing him to repentance and reconciliation with his father.

Ah ! how little that young man dreamt that his father so loved him ! And have not your thoughts about God been just the same ? You have tried to shut God out of your thoughts ; or, this being impossible, you have only thought of Him as One Who was angry with you.

How did you come to have such mistaken ideas ? If you only knew that He is longing to embrace you, and to assure you of his full and free forgiveness of all, and to tell you of all the bright inheritance which is waiting for you, if only you will claim it.

"But," you say, "I do not think peace is to be got so easily as all that. Do you mean to say that I may all at once believe that God loves me—and that all my sins are forgiven, because His Son has died in my stead—and so, **at once**, have peace and rest ?"

I mean it, or, rather, God means it ; for He says :

"The Son of God loved me, and gave Himself for me."

Yes ! peace is found—not by praying—not by repenting—not by reforming—not by feeling—but first by hearing, then believing God's message—by simply realizing what Jesus had already done for you.

More than a Friend

I WAS deeply interested in hearing of an incident that took place at a soldier's grave in one of the Southern States of America. A person was seen decking it with flowers; and a stranger observing him, asked, with a tone of sympathy, if his son were buried there. "No," was the reply. "A brother?" "No." "Some other relation?" "No." "**Whose memory** then, may I venture to ask, do you thus so sacredly and tenderly cherish?" Pausing a moment from emotion, he replied—"When the war broke out, I was drafted for the army; and, as I was unable to procure a substitute, I prepared to go. Just as I was leaving home to report myself for duty, a young man whom I knew came to me, and said: 'You have a large family, whom your wife cannot support when you are gone. I am a single man, and have no one depending upon me—I will go for you.' He went. In the battle of Chickamauga the poor fellow was dangerously wounded, died, and was buried here. Ever since his death I have wished to visit this place, and, having saved sufficient funds, I arrived yesterday, and to-day have found his grave."

The touching story concluded, he planted the rest of the flowers. Then taking a board, he inserted it at the foot of the grave. On it were written these simple words, and no more—

"He died for me"

I know your heart will glow when you think of that noble fellow's generous, self-sacrificing love for his friend. Does it not glow when you think of One who died for **YOU**? Is **that** deed forgotten, and not one loving, grateful thought given to His dear memory? As that generous soldier died to save his friend, so truly did Jesus die for you—yes, far more so. The soldier might have returned safe, but Jesus **knew** he went forth to death for you. And how have you treated Him?

He knew you did not love Him, nor even care for your own soul; but He saw you would be lost, so He gave Himself up to suffer in your stead. You have shed no tears for Him, nor experienced one loving feeling.

Perhaps you think that because He was the Son of God, He could feel no pain or grief! Listen! He said, "My soul is exceeding sorrowful, even unto death."—"If it be possible, let this cup pass from Me." He died a most suffering, agonizing death. and a mocking crowd stood round Him—

and, **all for you.**

JUST STOP DOING

YES, just stop doing, and begin to trust Christ to do ALL, and you are safe. A man is rowing a boat on a river just above a dreadful cataract. The current begins to bear him downward, the spectators on the banks give him up for lost; "He is gone!" they all exclaim. But in another moment a rope is thrown towards the wretched man; it strikes the water close to the boat. Now, how does the case stand? Do all the spectators call upon him to row harder to reach the shore? Oh, no; their eager, united cry is, *"Drop your oars! Catch hold of the rope!"* So all the sinner's hope lies not in struggling to save himself, but in ceasing to struggle; for while he tries to accomplish the work of salvation, he will not look to Christ to do it for him. It is not *doing*, but *yielding*, that is required.

THIS I did for THEE

"I GAVE My life for thee;
My precious blood I shed,
That thou might'st ransomed be,
And quickened from the dead.
I gave My life for thee—
What hast thou given for Me?

"I suffered much for thee—
More than thy tongue can tell—
Of bitterest agony,
To rescue thee from hell.
I suffered much for thee:
What canst thou bear for Me?

"And I have brought to Thee,
Down from My home above,
Salvation full and free,
My pardon and My love.
Great gifts I brought to thee:
What hast thou brought to Me?

"Oh, let thy life be given,
Thy years for Me be spent;
World-fetters all be riven,
And joys with suffering blent.
Give thou thyself to Me,
And I will welcome thee."

F. R. Havergal.

God's Answers to Your Questions

I AM young yet, and likely to live. I hardly need think of these things yet (?)

God says: "Boast not thyself of to-morrow; for thou knowest not what a day may bring forth" (Prov. 27. 1).

If I do die, shall I not be done with?

"The rich man died, and was buried; and in hell he lifted up his eyes, being in torments" (Luke 16. 22).

But I suppose it will be determined at the judgment day who will be sent there?

"He that believeth not is condemned **already** because he hath not believed in the name of the only begotten Son of God" (John 3. 18).

But I have lived a comparatively harmless life; am I condemned?

God says: "There is none righteous, no, not one" (Romans 3. 10). "Except a man be **born again**, he cannot see the kingdom of God" (John 3. 3).

God is a merciful God, and I trust that He will pass over my many misdeeds.

"He will by no means clear the guilty" (Ex. 34. 7). "Because I have called, and ye refused, I also will laugh when your fear cometh" (Prov. 1. 24).

But I say my prayers, and have given to God's work ; surely that will count in my favour ?

" Many shall say to Me in that day . . . we have done many wonderful works.—I never knew you, depart from Me " (Matt. 7. 22).

Why put me on the same level as the drunkard or social outcast ?

God says : " By one man sin entered into the world, and death by sin ;—all have sinned " (Rom. 5. 12).—" All we, like sheep, have gone astray." (Isa. 53. 6).

I cannot credit that I and the immoral are alike before God.

" Whosoever shall keep the whole law, and yet offend in one point, he is guilty of all " (James 2. 10).

If that be the case, I must plead guilty. I have sinned. What must I do to be saved ?

" Believe on the Lord Jesus Christ, and thou shalt be saved " (Acts 16. 31).

Tell me exactly what I am to believe.

That " The Lord hath laid on Him the iniquity of us all " (Isa. 53. 6). " He gave Himself for me " (Gal. 2. 20). " The just for the unjust " (1 Pet. 3. 18).

But must I do nothing to gain salvation ?

" A man is not justified by the works of the law ; but by the faith of Jesus Christ " (Gal. 2. 16).

I have believed from my earliest years that Jesus died, and rose again, and yet I am not saved.

" If thou shalt confess with thy mouth the Lord Jesus, and shalt believe **in thine heart** that God hath raised Him from the dead, thou shalt be saved " (Rom. 10. 9).

But does not the Bible say, " Work out your own salvation " ?

Yes—when salvation is yours, but not until then. God says, " To him that worketh not, but believeth in Him that justifieth the ungodly, his faith is counted for righteousness " (Rom. 4. 5).

Has God to do nothing for me ?

" Without shedding of blood there is no remission " (Heb. 9. 22). St. Paul says, " He loved me, and gave Himself for me " (Gal. 2. 20). Could He do more ?

To be saved just by believing seems too simple.

" If He had bid thee do some great thing, wouldest thou not have done it ? how much rather then, when He saith to thee, Wash, and be clean " (2 Kings 5. 13). " Believe on the Lord Jesus Christ, and thou **shalt** be saved " (Acts 16. 31).

Does God really love me, before I am saved ?

" God commendeth His love toward us, in that, **while we were yet sinners**, Christ died for us " (Rom. 5. 8). " Hereby perceive we the love of God, because He laid down His life for us " (1 John 3. 16).

Then I often think I am too great a sinner to be saved.

" Come now, and let us reason together, saith the Lord : though your sins be as **scarlet** they shall be as white as snow ; though they be red like crimson, they shall be as wool " (Isa. 1. 18).

But I should have to make so many sacrifices if I became a Christian ?

" What is a man profited, if he shall gain the whole world, and lose his own soul ? " (Matt. 6. 26.)

Again, I should be unable to bear the scoffs of my acquaintances.

" My grace is sufficient for thee, for My strength is made perfect in weakness " (2 Cor. 12. 9). " I the Lord have called thee, I will keep thee " (Isa. 42. 6).

If I come to Him, perhaps I may afterward fall away, and be lost.

God says : " I give unto them eternal life ; and they shall never perish, neither shall any pluck them out of my hand " (John 10. 28).

Well, then, I can but believe that Jesus diea for me.

" These things have I written, . . . that ye may **know** that ye HAVE eternal life " (1 John 5. 13).

It seems too good to be true.

" It is impossible for God to lie " (Heb. 6. 18).

" By Him all that believe are justified from **all** things, from which ye could not be justified by the law of Moses " (Acts. 13. 29).

"What Must I Do To Be Saved?"

By SIR ARTHUR BLACKWOOD.

GOD has drawn many striking pictures of *salvation*, but none clearer than the story of the Passover in Egypt. The simplest answer to the all-important question, " What must I do to be saved ? "

The Israelites in Egypt were *helpless slaves*. Could not help themselves, nor devise a way of salvation. Exactly the condition to-day of the *unconverted* man ; who is the bond-slave of sin.

The judgment that was coming upon Egypt would have overtaken Israel, if God in His mercy had not provided a way of deliverance. And so with us : we are lying under the sentence of God, " by nature the *children of wrath* "—" *condemned already* " (John 3. 18).

Sentence is thus passed upon us, but not executed. It is passed as it was upon the Israelites in Egypt before God revealed the way of life ; and until we are *sheltered beneath the blood*, we are alike under the condemnation. The way of Israel's deliverance by the blood on their door posts, is a picture of God's way of salvation for us, for every sinner—by the blood of the Lord Jesus Christ. (Read Exodus 12th chapter.)

In Egypt a lamb was to be slain, and the blood was to be sprinkled on the two side posts and lintel of the doors of their houses. Each family was then to assemble within to eat the flesh of the lamb " roasted with fire " ; but it must be clearly observed that it was upon the fulfilment of but one particular that the salvation of the Israelites depended—the blood outside the door ;—for God had said, " *When I see the blood*, I will pass over you." We need be at no pains to discover what the blood of the lamb was meant to teach us. The type is so clear → the precious blood of Christ."

As the lamb was slain, and by its death saved the first-born of those on whose door posts blood was sprinkled,—*so*,—the Scriptures tell us that Christ, the Lamb of God, has " suffered for us, the just for the unjust," and that whosoever believeth in Him should never come into condemnation.

When an Israelite took the blood, and put it outside upon the door posts and lintel, and went into his house, he *took shelter under the blood.* The blood was over him, and the sword of the destroying angel could not that night smite through the blood.

In like manner the sinner to-day that trusts in Jesus has *sheltered* himself under the blood. He believes he is guilty, but God has said, " When I see the blood, I will pass over you." He trusts in Christ's death, **in his stead** to save him from wrath. He thus takes God's way of salvation, and he is safe.

The blood alone was Israel's safety. So with us, it is on the blood of Christ *alone* that salvation depends. *Only the blood.*

And *your* life must date from the moment of your actually trusting in the blood of Christ.

Is the Blood Sprinkled?

(If you have not read the 12th of Exodus, please do so.)

THE Jews tell a story in connection with that dreadful Passover night. A Jewish father had one little girl, about ten years old. She was his only child, and he was very fond of her. As the first-born child in that family, she would be the one to die if the angel's stroke should fall on their dwelling. Before going to sleep, she asked her father **if the blood had been sprinkled on the door posts.** He said it had been, and she fell asleep. But her sleep was disturbed. She woke several times through the evening, and each time she asked anxiously if it was all right about the blood. Assured that it was, she tried to sleep on, but in vain. A little before midnight she woke again, in great alarm. She asked her father to take her in his arms, and carry her outside the door that she might see the blood. He did so; but to his horror found that there was no blood on the door posts! It had been left to a servant to attend to it, and he had neglected it. Her father ran to get the blood, and sprinkled it on the door posts with his own hand. His child saw the blood, and knowing that they were safe, she went sweetly to sleep.

LIFE IN A LOOK

THERE is life in a look at the Crucified One,
There is life at this moment for thee;
Then look, sinner, look unto Him, and be saved;
Unto Him who was nailed to the tree.

Oh, why was He there as the bearer of sin,
If on Jesus **thy** sins were not laid?
Oh, why from His side flowed the sin-cleansing blood,
If His dying **thy** debt has not paid?

It is not thy tears of repentance or prayers,
But the **blood**, that atones for the soul;
On Him, then, who shed it, thou mayest at once
Thy weight of iniquities roll.

Then doubt not thy welcome, since God hath declared
There remaineth no more to be done;
That once in the end of the world He appeared,
And completed the work He begun;

But take, with rejoicing, from Jesus at once,
The life everlasting He gives;
And know, with assurance, thou never canst die,
Since Jesus thy Righteousness lives.

A Glorious Victory

"A VICTORY, a glorious victory!" shouted Horace Fleming. "Did not I tell you, uncle, that Old England never would be beaten? Though Frank is at the front he will be all right, you may be sure."

Frank Conyers was an only son of Mr. and Mrs. Conyers, heir to a considerable property. He had been educated carefully; and his parents had hoped he would eventually take his place as owner of a large inheritance. But Frank was filled with thoughts of military glory, and gave his parents no peace until they consented to his entering the army. His military career had been a short one; but now, amid the stirring scenes of the war, he was seeing the realities of a soldier's life, also its hardships. He had been wounded, and his parents fondly hoped that he would be satisfied now, and they had been anxiously looking for a letter announcing his speedy return home "invalided," when Horace Fleming rushed in, with the news of a glorious victory.

Mr. and Mrs. Conyers were so well acquainted with the courageous and daring spirit of their son, that they knew he would be an actor in the scene again, if able to mount his horse. But his wound had been so recent, they hoped he was still too unwell to make any such attempt.

Slowly passed the hours of suspense until the full information anxiously looked for, yet dreaded, was received; and then the shock was none the less when a letter from the War Office was received, in which these words were read: **"I am truly sorry to inform you, that on the 6th instant, in the desperate charge of the cavalry, your gallant son, Lieutenant Conyers, fell while bravely cheering on his men."**

They seemed to burn like letters of fire before their horror-stricken gaze. Thus the worst of their fears came upon them in all its sudden horror, and the bereaved parents were utterly prostrated beneath the blow. In vain well-meaning friends spoke comfort, but they sorrowed as those who have lost their all.

How fearful is affliction when the mourner cannot flee to Him who binds up the stricken heart ; when the bright hope of the Christian believer is unknown ! This was the grief that had fallen upon the unhappy parents of Frank Conyers. As their lives were of this world, worldly and with no thought, no hope beyond, bitter beyond expression was the agony of their grief.

The first transport of sorrow was succeeded by a sullen despair ; when their affliction was re-awakened by the arrival of the baggage and effects of an only son cruelly torn from them. In the agonies of her grief, the mother clasped the garments of their son which spoke to her so plainly of him. At last, as poor Frank's desk was lifted out of the packing case, Mr. Conyers seized it with a sudden hope that some last word from their son might be found within it.

As his trembling fingers sought for the key, and fitted it to the lock, how well he remembered the day on which he had given the desk to Frank for a birthday present, made after his own directions, with a secret drawer. After a moment's delay, caused by his shaking hands, the private drawer revealed to view a thick letter, addressed,

"To my beloved Father and Mother."

With a cry Mr. Conyers summoned his wife and with straining eyes they read together :—

"Dearest Father and Mother,—I am once more out of the doctor's hands and pronounced 'fit for duty'; and as I may now be called into action at a moment's warning, I write you a letter which will, should I fall, tell you my whole heart. I have often thought since I was wounded that if I had been killed instead of only wounded, you would not have had a last word from me to speak comfort to you. But could I have written then, how different would it have been: I should have told you that I died for the honour of my country, and tried to soothe your sorrow for my loss, by the thought that I had fallen gloriously on the battle-field. But now! oh, my loved ones, should I fall in the impending engagement, I shall die a victor through the blood of the Lamb, even Christ my Lord,—not an earthly victor, but victorious over death and the grave, my soul going with joy to meet the great Captain of my salvation.—I think I see your astonishment, dear parents, as these words meet your eyes; and I hasten to tell you how I came to have such views and feelings,—those hopes, nay, certainties, which fill me with a joy that is not of earth, even in expectation of a violent death.

"While I lay in the hospital, wounded, a brother officer, quite a young fellow, whom we used laughingly to call 'Praying Fred,' was brought in badly wounded, and placed in the next bed to mine; he had to undergo a painful operation, which he bore like a hero,—not a murmur then, or after, escaping from his lips,—although he suffered torturing pain. This showed me that he practised what he preached, and that there must be reality in the religion he professed. Some such thoughts were going through my mind, when I met his eyes suddenly raised to mine as I looked at him, the day after the operation had been performed, and though, thinking he was asleep, I could not forbear expressing them aloud, as he gazed at me in wonder at my earnest look.

" 'Oh, yes,' he said. 'My religion is a reality —a support and comfort under every trial. I know that nothing can occur to me without the eye of my heavenly Father taking notice of it ; and whatever He orders is right, and just what I would choose, if I could order things for myself, for I know that all things work together for good to those who love Him.'

" 'Why, what good can it do you to be laid there in torture, deprived of a limb ?' I asked in surprise.

"My companion was silent for a moment,—and then he replied : 'One good result is, that it has given me an opportunity to speak to you, friend, of the hope that is in me ; and if you are brought to know the blessedness of that hope, how joyful will it have been for me that I was laid here. How small a price would my lost limb and pain be, for the joy of knowing that I was instrumental in bringing you to a knowledge of my Lord and my Saviour. If (as we are told) one soul is worth more than the whole world, how trifling comparatively my sufferings, to the bliss of carrying the good news of salvation to you.'

" 'You must not value me at so high a price as the "whole world," even though I am an only son,' I said, laughing ; for the conversation was becoming too serious for my worldly mind.

" 'Oh, Conyers !' he replied, 'you mistake ; it was not I who set that value upon you ; the Creator of us all showed that He did so value you, when He gave "HIS only Son" to die for you, that you might live for ever.'

"Dear parents! when Fred Singleton spoke those words, a veil seemed to fall from before my eyes. I thought of you and of your indulgent love for me. I knew that you would give up your lives, before you would suffer me to fall. And then I thought of God giving **His** Son to die for me. In a moment I saw, as by a sudden revelation, how dreadful must be my state as a sinner, to require such sacrifice;—and how wonderful must be the love of God to me, to give His only Son to die in my stead. All the sermons I had ever heard,—'to come to Jesus and be saved,'—seemed to rise up in array before me, as I lay stunned by the suddenness of the revelation that swept through my brain. At length, as though compelled to speak, I said, 'Singleton, you have struck me to the heart; if God has so valued my soul,—(as I now see and feel He has)—**what a fool I have been not to value it more myself.** I never saw it in that light; in fact (to be sincere) I never thought about my soul at all.'

"'That is it;—that is the danger,'—said Singleton. 'We forget that we have within these bodies, spirits that can never die; and yet, how awful to think that at any moment the body may cease to exist, and its immortal tenant go on its eternal journey, unsaved, to everlasting misery. Oh! why do we go on facing such a doom, when Christ shed His blood for us?'

"'God must be very angry with us for neglecting to seek Him,' I said, thinking aloud.

"'He pities us and entreats us to believe and be saved,' said Singleton, tenderly. 'You believe that Jesus died for you; do you not?'

"'Yes; oh, yes,' I replied.

" 'Then, my friend, God asks no more from you.'

" 'How do you mean? Oh, Singleton, explain this to me more fully,' I exclaimed.

" 'I have heard it explained in this way, Conyers; it is simple, but I think perfect,' said Singleton. 'If a man was drowning and a rope was thrown to him, his seeing the rope and that it was intended he should grasp it and be saved, would not of itself save him,—he might perish in sight of the means of safety; but if he grasped the rope and clung to it for life, then he would be safe; don't you see? You must take the salvation Christ has secured for you, over eighteen hundred years ago; it is for you; only believe it; accept this salvation, and you have done your part. God has given His Son, the Saviour, Christ has given Himself for you, and you have only to believe that He did so, and that God has accepted that sacrifice,—in your place.'

"Oh! I see it—**I see it all now** and I felt compelled to cry out, 'It is marvellous, but it is true. I feel it;—I know it. I do believe that Christ has died for me, and that I am thus saved—yes, saved for ever!'

" 'Bless the Lord for this great salvation!' cried Singleton, as well as his feeble voice would permit. 'Did I not say right, that all things work together for our good if we love Him? How little I thought when I was laid here what a blessing was in store for me!'—His voice became exhausted, and I begged him not to weaken himself by speaking any more just then.

"The next day he was very faint, only exchanging an occasional word or look with me, but they were truly words and looks from the borders of the heavenly land to which he was hastening. Not even the painful amputation could save his life ; and the doctors at last reluctantly admitted the fact, when he asked them calmly if it was not so. After they had left him, he turned to me and said, 'Here is a leaflet which has been my motto since I knew the Saviour ; let it be yours.—Never forget it.' He pressed my hand as he placed the leaflet in it. I send a copy of the verses, that you also, dear ones, may make it your motto :—

'JESUS ! and shall it ever be
A mortal man ashamed of Thee ?—
Ashamed of Thee, whom angels praise,
Whose glories shine through endless days ?

Ashamed of Jesus ! yes, I may,
When I've no guilt to wash away ;
No tears to wipe, no good to crave,
No fears to quell, no soul to save.

Till then—nor is my boasting vain—
Till then, I boast a Saviour slain ;
And oh, may this my glory be,
That Christ is not ashamed of me ! '

"The next day it was plain that my dear—yes, doubly dear, friend was sinking ; but still he met my gaze with a bright smile and an upward look, as he said repeatedly, 'I am going home.' Towards evening he said, 'All things work together for good to those who love Him. See, the loss of this limb is sending me home to that home. I might have passed many years of suffering on earth, but my gracious Father wills it otherwise ; He is taking me home to be with Himself.' Those were his last words, as he sank into a sleep, and awoke no more.

"Dear parents, since I have left the hospital I have boldly taken my stand as a soldier of the Cross; and should I die upon the field of battle, without a moment's warning, remember that to me sudden death will be sudden glory, for I shall be with my Saviour, and with Singleton once more. When you read these lines, believe that it is I, your son, your loving son, speaking; and even from heaven let my voice reach you,—for it is my voice, not the silent pen. I am not dead; I live! Because my Saviour lives, I live;—and I implore of you, beloved ones, hear me, that you also may with me enjoy the blessings of His kingdom. Never think of me as if dead,—only having gone before you, called away by God in His mercy, that you may be led to see His love, and to believe in Him as I believed when Singleton spoke to me. Remember how much greater a love must God have had for His 'only and well-beloved Son' than even you, dear parents, could possibly have felt for me. And then think how much He must have loved us, when He gave His only Son to suffer for our sins. Take Him for **your** Saviour; for we shall be for ever together. Come to Him now, is the prayer of your DEVOTED SON."

Had a voice indeed sounded in their ears from the eternal world, the awe, mingled with rapture (that fell upon Mr. and Mrs. Conyers, as they read these lines) could not have been surpassed. With one consent, they sank upon their knees together and accepted the Saviour of their son to be their Saviour—a Glorious Victory!

A NOBLE ROMAN

I DARE say some of you have heard the story about a young Roman that had been condemned to death. He had been guilty of treason, and condemned by the judges to die, when up stepped a brother, an older one, who had served in his country's wars, and had both his arms cut off. This brother, standing before the judges, holding up the stumps of his arms, pleaded for his brother's life; **not** for what his brother had done, **but for what he had done.** He confessed that his brother was guilty; he confessed that his brother was worthy of death; but for what he had done in the service of his country, he pleaded that his brother's life might be spared. And looking on what the brother had done, the judges for his sake pardoned the guilty brother. Ah, that is just what Christ does for us sinners. Christ died on Calvary that we might live. **We** deserved death; but for the sake of Christ, and because He laid down His life that we might live, God pardons our sins.

Reformation Useless IF thou art not born again, all thy outward reformation is naught in the sight of God; thou hast shut the door with the thief still in the house.

Redemption that is in Christ Jesus (Rom. 3. 24)

"THUS saith the Lord: Behold I set before you the Way of Life and the Way of Death (Jer. 21. 8). I call Heaven and earth to record this day against you,—that I have set before you Life and death. Therefore **choose Life**—that thou mayest love the Lord" (Deut. 31. 19).

"For God so loved the world that He gave His only begotten Son, that whosoever believeth in Him should not perish but have everlasting life. Eternal life,—and they shall never perish" (John 10. 28 and 3. 16).

"Herein is love, not that we loved God, but that He loved us, and sent His Son to be the propitiation for our sins" (1 John 4. 10).

"While we were yet sinners, Christ died for us" (Rom. 5. 8) ——→ "the ungodly" (Rom. 5. 6).

"The Just for the unjust" (1 Pet. 3. 18).

"Redeemed with the precious blood of Christ" (1 Pet. 1. 18). "We have peace with God" (Rom. 5. 1).

"What shall we then say to these things? If God be for us, who can be against us? He that spared not His own Son, but delivered Him up for us all, how shall He not with Him also freely give us all things?" (Rom. 8. 31).

Read 3rd chapter of St. John,
and then Romans 3. 19 to 8. 39.

The Amended Will

A FEW days ago, I was asked to dine with an elderly gentleman, over whose head seventy summers had passed. He had been known as a Christian for many years, but, as we often find, had allowed his ideas of humility to hinder the joy of "full assurance" of salvation. At the same time, his self-denying labours of love, and close following in the footsteps of the Divine Master, would shame many advanced believers.

As he sat in his arm-chair, in the course of the evening, he said, "I am going to the Continent to-morrow, and as we never know what a day may bring forth, especially at my time of life, I have written out a few directions as to the disposal of my property, and wish you to append your name as having witnessed my signature."

He then read the will over to me, and I was particularly struck with the concise way in which he had given expression to his wishes. There was nothing superfluous or vague, and nothing omitted. With the following words he concluded: "*I wish to testify that I die trusting in the merits of my Lord and Saviour Jesus Christ, and hope* I am accepted for His sake."

I said, "You have stated everything so clearly, may I ask why you add, '**I hope** I am accepted'? The Word of God tells us that He **hath** made us accepted in the Beloved; and again, 'We **know** (*not hope*) that if our earthly house of this tabernacle were dissolved, we have a building of God, an house . . . eternal in the heavens'" (2 Cor. 5. 1).

"Well," said he, "it is one thing for St. Paul to speak thus, and another for me. I have no sympathy with those who are presumptuous enough to speak so confidently about their salvation. They must be sadly wanting in humility."

"Friend," I replied, "if it be presumption, has not God endorsed it? Did not Christ say, 'He that heareth My Word, and believeth on Him that sent Me, **hath** everlasting life, and shall not come into condemnation, but **is** passed from death unto life ' (John 5. 24). You say you trust in the merit and work of Christ, and Him alone."

"I do," he added, "firmly believing that when He said, 'It is finished,' the work was fully done, and nothing can be added to it." "Or taken away?" I inquired. "I see," he replied, "you do not believe in the final perseverance of the saints."

"I believe rather," said I, "in the final perseverance of God to guard and keep His saints unto the end. If it depended upon the holiest saint of God to keep himself, it would be a sorry affair. He could not stand for half an hour. It is the perseverance of the Father in drawing all to Jesus,—the perseverance of the Son and the Holy Ghost in keeping them. Is not this a firm basis on which to rest?" "It is indeed a sure foundation," he exclaimed. "I see, I see my mistake. It is far more presumptuous to doubt God, than to take Him at His Word"; and he struck out the word "hope" and inserted "know."

The Wondrous Story

I WILL sing the wondrous story
Of the Christ who died for me;
How He left His home in glory,
For the cross on Calvary.

Yes, I'll sing the wondrous story
Of the Christ who died for me;
Sing it with the saints in glory,
Gathered by the crystal sea.

I was lost; but Jesus found me—
Found the sheep that went astray;
Threw His loving arms around me,
Drew me back into His way.

Perfection and Power

NO honour like a relation to Christ; no riches like the graces of Christ; no learning like the knowledge of Christ; and no persons like the servants of Christ. Think not the worse of Him for His manger or His cross. As He ceaseth not to be **man** in His highest estate, so He was **GOD** in His lowest. His words were oracles, His works, miracles. His life was a pattern; His death a sacrifice; His resurrection triumphant; His coming again will be magnificent. All the angels in heaven adore Him; all the devils in hell fear Him; all the redeemed have been saved by Him; all the lost shall be judged by Him.

White as the Driven Snow

"YOU say a man can know that his sins are forgiven! No, never! If a man were pure as the running stream, or white as the driven snow, he might; but for mortal man to know that his sins are forgiven is presumption." So said a man to one who had been urging that sin was forgiven once and for ever through the Blood of the Atonement.

But is it so? Which is right? Can a man lie down on his bed at night and feel a positive certainty that his sin is put away, and that if he died in his sleep, or was shot to-morrow, his sin would not be reckoned against him?

What does God's Book say:—

> "There is no condemnation to them that are in Christ Jesus. Rom. 8. 1. I have caused thine iniquity to pass from thee. Zech. 3. 4. Justified freely by His grace. Rom. 3. 24. He that believeth hath everlasting life, and shall not come into condemnation; but is passed from death unto life. John 5. 24. Their sins and iniquities will I remember no more. Heb. 10. 17. As far as the east is from the west, so far hath He removed our transgressions from us. Ps. 103. 12. I have blotted out as a thick cloud thy transgressions. Isa. 44. 22."

Many more of God's own words might be added, all proving that it is not any presumption to know whom we believe, and be confident that He is both willing and able to present us faultless before His Father at the Great Day.

He who only says: "I hope I am saved," cannot be happy in the fullest sense of the term, nor is he in the position that God would have him to be.

Assurance of Salvation

GOD'S own words:—"This is the covenant . . . their sins and iniquities will I remember no more. Now where remission of these is, there is no more offering for sin. Having therefore, brethren, boldness to enter into the holiest by the blood of Jesus, . . . let us draw near with full assurance of faith. An oath for confirmation is to men an end of all strife. Wherein God, willing more abundantly to shew to the heirs of promise the immutability of His counsel, confirmed it by an oath; that by two immutable things (in which it was impossible for God to lie) we might have a strong consolation who have fled for refuge to lay hold upon the hope set before us; which hope we have as an **anchor** of the soul both **sure and steadfast**" (Heb. 6. 16-20). "These things are written unto you that believe on the name of the Son of God, that ye may **know that ye have** eternal life" (1 John 5. 13).

Cleopatra's Needle

THIRTY-THREE centuries ago—says Mr. Canton, in his history of the Bible Society—Cleopatra's Needle was cut in the red granite quarries of Syene. Under clouds of gnats, and driven hard by rods of taskmasters, long files of captives dragged this enormous column on sledges to the sacred river, while gangs of water-carriers poured a flood of water under the runners to keep the groaning wood from catching fire. It was then floated down the Nile on a ship, and erected with infinite labour before the splendid heathen Temple of the Sun, in the "city of On." A great many years ago the English got permission to move it, and at great expense to carry it away to London. It had to be built into a small iron ship or barge on the spot, and, after getting it into the sea, it was tugged round from the Mediterranean through the Bay of Biscay to London, and this wonderful Cleopatra's Needle was raised upon its pedestal on the Thames Embankment. In the pedestal was placed a jar containing copies of the Bible in four languages, and also one particular verse in two hundred and fifteen languages.

Is it not strange that after a lapse of three millenniums (**3000 years**) the Bible should have been committed to the care of this same great obelisk, whose gold-capped summit flashed out to the far pastures of Goshen in an age in which the story of Exodus had scarcely yet begun? It is, indeed, yet not more strange and wondrous than the whole story of the Book,—the Bible.

We ask, with deep curiosity, what was the verse, translated into **two hundred and fifteen languages**, and deposited in its pedestal. Why, it is the best known verse in the whole Bible, and more used in bringing blessings to souls than any other in the Scripture. Once called "The Bible in miniature." Here it is:—

> **"For God so loved the world that He gave His only begotten Son, that whosoever believeth in Him should not perish, but have everlasting life."**
>
> **John 3. 16.**

Spurning the Remedy

A MAN said to me not long ago, " Do you think there is any justice in my being condemned because a man sinned six thousand years ago ? I don't believe a word of it." Now let me say, there will be no one lost on account of Adam's sin. But I hear someone say, " That's a plain contradiction. You have said we should be, and now you tell me we shall not be."

Let me see if I can illustrate it. Suppose I am dying of some terrible disease, and I am given up by the physicians, who say I must die. But there comes a man whom I have known for years, and he says, " You are a dying man ! " I say to him, " I know it ; I don't want any one to tell me that." He says to me, " But there is a remedy." I say, " I don't believe there's any remedy ; I have tried all the leading physicians, and they say there is no hope."

" I tell you there is a remedy ! " says he ; " twenty years ago I was as far gone as yourself, and I was given up by all the physicians to die, but I took that medicine (and he holds it out to me), and it cured me. Listen now—there is the medicine, it shall not cost you a farthing ; just take it, and you will get well." But I do not take it, though I have every reason to believe the man is speaking the truth. To be sure I shall die, but that is not the reason why I die ; it is because I spurn the remedy. And if men die eternally it will not be God's fault, but because they have despised the remedy. They are not lost because they are sinners, but because they rejected the Saviour.

"I May be Dead To-morrow"

AN earnest Christian doctor one day called to see an old man that he had frequently visited before. Many a time had Dr. S—— spoken faithfully to old John and his wife about their souls' salvation ; but apparently without result.

Old John listened attentively, and tacitly agreed to the truth set before him; but seemed always to avoid coming to the point.

He would willingly admit that he was a sinner,—that he stood in need of God's salvation. He would even declare his intention of some day seeking the Saviour. He wished to be saved, indeed, but simply to escape the punishment of hell. He intended to prepare for heaven, but would put off till what seemed to him " a more convenient season."

Old John was suffering from an attack of bronchitis. His life was not in danger ; but he felt painfully weak and ill.

Dr. S—— made the necessary inquiries, and, after promising to get some medicine ready, when called for, he was about to say " good-bye," when John's wife inquired : " When must John take the physic, sir ? "

" I will put the directions on the label," replied Dr. S—— ; then with a

smile he turned to the invalid and said: "Let me see; you are not very ill; supposing you begin to take the medicine this day month."

"This day month, sir?"—cried both at once, in astonishment.

"Yes—why not? Is that too soon?"

"Too soon! why, sir, I may be dead then!" said John.

"That is true; but you must remember, you really are not very bad yet. Still, perhaps you had better begin to take it in a week."

"But, sir," cried John, in great perplexity; "beggin' your pardon, sir, I mightn't live a week."

"Of course you may not, John; but very likely you will, and the medicine will be in the house; it will keep, and if you should find yourself getting worse, you could take some. I shan't charge anything for it. If you should feel worse to-morrow even, you might begin then."

"Sir, I may be dead to-morrow! I hope you won't be angry with me, nor think me ungrateful to you, as have al'ays been so good to me; but you know, sir, I don't want to get worse; and though I'll war'nt the physic be good stuff, it'll do me no good while 'tis in the bottle; and it do seem to me, sir, as 'tis goin' against reason to put off takin' it."

"When would you propose to begin then, John ?"

"Well, sir, I thought you'd tell me to begin to-day."

"Begin to-day by all means," said Dr. S——, kindly. "I only wanted to show you how false your own reasoning is, when you put off taking the medicine which the Great Physician has provided for your sin-sick soul. Just think how long you have neglected the remedy He has provided. For years you have turned away from the Lord Jesus. You have said to yourself, 'next week,' or 'next year,' or 'when I am on my death-bed, I will seek the Lord'; any time rather than the present. And yet the present is the only time that you are sure of. God's offer is only for 'to-day.' 'Now is the accepted time; behold, now is the day of salvation' (2 Cor. 6. 2). I need not tell you how ready the Lord Jesus is to receive you; how His precious blood was shed for you. You have the medicine, so to speak, in your hands; but, to use your own argument, it will do you no good unless you take it; and it is foolish to put this off, even until to-morrow."

Old John's eyes were full of tears as he pressed the hand of his kind friend.

"Plain speakin'," he remarked to his wife; "but I reckon he's right, old woman; I never saw it just the same before."

The Wondrous Cross

When I survey the wondrous cross
On which the Prince of Glory died,
My richest gain I count but loss,
And pour contempt on all my pride.

Forbid it, Lord, that I should boast,
Save in the death of Christ my God:
All the vain things that charm me most,
I sacrifice them to His blood.

See! from His head, His hands, His feet,
Sorrow and love flow mingled down!
Did e'er such love and sorrow meet,
Or thorns compose so rich a crown?

Were the whole realm of nature mine,
That were an off'ring far too small:
Love so amazing, so divine,
Demands my life, my soul, my all.

My Sins Deserve Eternal Death

By Canon DYSON HAGUE, London, Ontario, Canada

ONE Sunday evening, when I was Rector of St. Paul's Church, Halifax, "the Westminster Abbey of Canada," I told, towards the close of my sermon, the following story :—Many years ago, Dr. Valpy, a well-known English scholar, wrote a verse of four lines as the longing of his heart and the confession of his faith. This was the simple stanza :

"In peace let me resign my breath,
And Thy salvation see ;
My sins deserve eternal death,
But Jesus died for me."

Later on he gave this verse to his friend, Dr. Marsh, the author of the Life of *Captain Hedley Vicars,* and the verse became a great blessing to him. Dr. Marsh gave the lines to his friend, Lord Roden, who was so impressed with them that he got Dr. Marsh to write them out, and then fastened the paper over the mantelpiece in his study. There, yellow with age, they hung for years, a memorial of the beloved hand.

Some time after this, an old friend —General Taylor, one of the heroes of

Waterloo—came to visit him at Tollymore Park. Lord Roden noticed that the eyes of the old veteran were always fixed for a few moments on the motto over the mantelpiece. " Why, General," said Lord Roden, " you will soon know those lines by heart."

" I know them now by heart," replied the General, with feeling,—and those simple words were the means of bringing him to know the way of salvation. Some two years afterwards the physician, who had been with the old General while he lay a-dying, wrote to Lord Roden to say that his friend had gone, and that his last words were some words he had learned to love in his lifetime; they were:

" In peace let me resign my breath,
And Thy salvation see;
My sins deserve eternal death,
But Jesus died for me."

Years afterwards, at the house of a neighbour, Lord Roden happened to tell the story of the old General and these lines, and among those who heard it was a young officer in the British Army. He listened carelessly enough. A few months later, however, Lord Roden received a message from the officer that he wanted to see him, as he was in a rapid decline. As the Earl entered the

sickroom the dying officer extended both his hands, repeating :

> **" In peace let me resign my breath,**
> **And Thy salvation see ;**
> **My sins deserve eternal death,**
> **But Jesus died for me."**

" Those simple words," he added, " have been God's message of peace and comfort to my heart in this illness."

◈ ◈ ◈

WHAT a Friend we have in Jesus
All our sins and griefs to bear !
What a privilege to carry
Everything to God in prayer !
Oh, what peace we often forfeit,
Oh, what needless pain we bear—
All because we do not carry
Everything to God in prayer !

Have we trials and temptations ?
Is there trouble anywhere ?
We should never be discouraged ;
Take it to the Lord in prayer !
Can we find a Friend so faithful,
Who will all our sorrows share ?
Jesus knows our every weakness—
Take it to the Lord in prayer.

Conversations with Christ

IF I were asked what is the thing the devil, the world, and the flesh try hardest to prevent Christians from getting, I should reply, "Conversations with Christ." I say this from my own experience, and that of others.—A quiet unhurried speaking with Jesus alone, and hearing His replies—this is what every Christian needs daily, or to get in the still hours of the night. Perhaps some may only get it once a week or hardly ever. If you are a Christian, do stop and ask yourself, "When did I last so talk with Christ?"

★ ★ ★ ★

It is so easy to go to services—listen to prayers, sing, or pray with others, without realizing the presence of the Lord Jesus Christ. Communion services are not necessarily conversations with Christ, nor preaching, teaching, or working for Him. You may even be busy all day about God's matters, give time, money or thought to His work, and yet never converse with or consult Him about your pleasures and difficulties. The danger is great. —You will get cold, and even stray—but more than that, when you meet Him in the hereafter will wake up to the fact that you and your Saviour are almost strangers. It will be a horrible surprise to you that nothing should remain of all the work on which you spent your life, for " without Me ye can do nothing," had been forgotten by you.

He meant that you should have talked to Him continually about everything you did, and should have been always conscious of His sympathy and oversight. But instead of that, you talked only to men and women, and made shift with their advice, sympathy and help. He meant you to have asked His counsel about that money trouble. He would have arranged it all ; but you only asked your lawyer, and it turned out badly. He meant you to have told Him your anxieties about your son, and He would have ended them ; but you only consulted your friend, and matters got worse and worse. He meant you to have asked Him for light about that doctrine which you could not understand ; but you went to books to get it explained, and you became more uncertain than before ; He would have satisfied you. He meant you to have confessed to Him that secret sin, and He would have forgiven you and cleansed you ; but you confessed it to your clergyman or minister, and it torments you to this hour. He meant you to have asked Him how much money you were to give away ; but you settled that yourself, and settled it wrong. He would have been your counsellor about the profession you chose, the situation you accepted, the servant you engaged, the books you read, the friendships you formed ; but you chose other counsellors, and all has been failure.

May the Holy Spirit strike the scales from your eyes Now, and may you take Christ as your Personal Friend and Counsellor.

THE LAST CALL

Again to those who have not yet decided

"Come now, and let us reason together, saith the Lord; though your sins be as scarlet, they shall be as white as snow; though they be red like crimson, they shall be as wool" (Isa. 1. 18).

"Herein is love, not that we loved God, but that He loved us, and sent His Son to be the propitiation for our sins" (1 John 4. 10).

"While we were yet sinners, Christ died for us" (Rom. 5. 8).

JUST as I am—without one plea,
But that Thy blood was shed for me,
And that Thou bid'st me come to Thee,
O Lamb of God, I come, I come!

Just as I am—poor, wretched, blind,
Sight, riches, healing of the mind;
Yea, all I need, in Thee to find—
O Lamb of God, I come, I come!

Just as I am—Thou wilt receive,
Wilt welcome, pardon, cleanse, relieve:
Because Thy promise I believe—
O Lamb of God, I come, I come!

Just as I am—Thy love unknown
Has broken every barrier down;
Now to be Thine, yea, Thine alone—
O Lamb of God, I come, I come!

THE MARKED TESTAMENT

---

200 *Verses marked in Red.*

The Object is to direct attention to simple and definite Gospel Texts, which, under the Holy Spirit's teaching, help to make plain God's Way of Salvation through Christ.

Sample copy (in English or French) sent post free to any address on receipt of 8*d.* *in stamps ; or in*

Moroccoette Yapp binding, 2*s.*
French Morocco Limp, 2*s.* 6*d.*
French Morocco Yapp, 3*s.*

SCRIPTURE PORTIONS

with the same markings as above :
John, with parts of Acts and Romans,
John and Hebrews,
Mark and Romans,
all 2d. each.

THE TRAVELLER'S GUIDE

English Edition, 6d.
Same size bound in leather, 2s.
Reduction for quantities.

Issued in 21 languages, including Chinese, Dutch, French, German, Italian, Japanese, Russian, and Spanish, etc.

That the book may be read as widely as possible, a sample copy will be sent post free to any address in Great Britain, on receipt of 7d. in stamps.

GOSPEL BOOKLETS

8 *and* 12 *pages.*

Attractive, clear and pointed messages, useful for Mission, Open Air, Hospital, and other branches of Christian Work.

ONE HALFPENNY EACH

Sample Packet 50 *for* 2s.

These Booklets are also made up in assorted packets containing 12 different titles, 6d., by post 7d.; 3 different packets, 1/8 post free.

Many of the stories in the Traveller's Guide are to be found in this Series. A list of titles and samples can be had on application.

My Decision.

I Confess myself to be a sinner before God, and worthy of Eternal death.

I Believe the Lord Jesus Christ to be the Substitute who bore my sin and its penalty.

I Accept Him as my personal Saviour ; and—

I Thank Him for the forgiveness of my sins, and I trust Him for grace to live a holy life.

Name ....

Date ....

(?) *IF I found a gold piece in the road, certainly I should tell the first friend I met.—If I heard unexpectedly that some old relative had left me a fortune, large or small,—it would be hard to keep it in. Yes, or any other good news. Can I then help telling my friends of the Saviour that I have found,—and making sure that HE is theirs also? Even if I cannot see them all, or speak to any of them, I can read, or lend this book to others.*